BERLIN

By Frederic V. Grunfeld
and the Editors of Time-Life Books

With photographs by Leonard Freed

THE GREAT CITIES · TIME-LIFE BOOKS · AMSTERDAM

The Author: Frederic V. Grunfeld was born in Berlin in 1929 but educated in Switzerland, England and the United States. A graduate of both the University of Chicago and Columbia University, he began his career as a music critic and radio broadcaster in New York City. During the 1960s, while serving as European Cultural Correspondent for the *Reporter* magazine, he paid frequent visits to Berlin to cover its theatrical and musical renaissance. His books include *The Art and Times of the Guitar*, and a social history of Nazism, *The Hitler File*.

The Photographer: Leonard Freed, born in New York City in 1929, has produced a number of photographic books, including *Deutsche Juden Heute (German Jews Today)*, *Black and White in America* and *Made in Germany*. He covered the Arab-Israeli wars of 1967 and 1973, and has contributed to the London *Sunday Times*, the *New York Times* and West Germany's *Stern* magazine. He has also held several one-man exhibitions in Europe and the United States.

EDITOR: Dale Brown
Design Consultant: Louis Klein
Picture Editor: Pamela Marke
Assistant Picture Editor: Anne Angus

Editorial Staff for *Berlin*:
Deputy Editors: Christopher Farman, Simon Rigge
Designer: Graham Davis
Staff Writers: Mike Brown, Deborah Thompson
Picture Researcher: Gunn Brinson
Text Researchers: Susan Dawson, Vanessa Kramer, Elizabeth Loving
Design Assistant: Shirin Patel

Editorial Production for the Series:
Art Department: Julia West
Editorial Department: Ellen Brush, Molly Sutherland, Betty H. Weatherley
Picture Department: Thelma Gilbert, Christine Hinze, Brigitte Guimpier

The captions and text of the picture essays were written by the staff of TIME-LIFE Books.

Published by TIME-LIFE International (Nederland) B.V. Ottho Heldringstraat 5, Amsterdam 1018.

Cover: the massive Brandenburg Gate, surmounted by a four-horsed chariot bearing the Goddess of Victory, forms a sombre silhouette against the sky. Built in 1791 by Carl Gotthard Langhans, the gate now stands just inside the Eastern half of Berlin, a nostalgic symbol of past glories.

First end paper: layers of posters plastered on a news and advertising pillar in East Berlin have peeled away over the years to leave a curled and cryptic collage of announcements.

Last end paper: fine mist softens the formal contours of the Charlottenburg Palace gardens in West Berlin. Designed in the baroque style, the palace and its grounds were started in 1695 for Sophie Charlotte, The Electress of Brandenburg.

TIME LIFE BOOKS

THE WORLD'S WILD PLACES
HUMAN BEHAVIOUR
THE ART OF SEWING
THE OLD WEST
THE EMERGENCE OF MAN
LIFE LIBRARY OF PHOTOGRAPHY
TIME-LIFE LIBRARY OF ART
FOODS OF THE WORLD
GREAT AGES OF MAN
LIFE SCIENCE LIBRARY
LIFE NATURE LIBRARY

Contents

I

A Sundered City

With any other city, you might begin by writing about the people, the architecture, the atmosphere. Here in Berlin you have to begin and end with politics. It is a political landscape, as fascinating in its way as anything that Nature has created in the Rockies or the Himalayas. Perhaps nowhere else in the world are political cause and effect quite so visible to the naked eye as in this utterly improbable city that used to be known as "Athens on the River Spree". Step to the windows of one of the modern office buildings near the old centre of Berlin and you can take in all of the historical contradictions at a single glance.

In the distance, above the treetops of the Tiergarten, gleams the golden figure of an immense Winged Victory, celebrating a series of Prussian military triumphs over the French, the Danes, the Austrians, the Bavarians; the statue's 200-foot column is ringed with the barrels of French cannon captured during the Franco-Prussian war of 1870-71.

Near by, at the northern edge of the park, stands the domed, ornate Reichstag building, home of the German parliament until 1933, when the notorious Reichstag fire, widely believed to have been started by the Nazis themselves, gave Hitler the excuse he needed to clamp an iron grip on the whole of Germany. After more than 30 years as a ruin, the burned-out building has been carefully restored to serve as, among other things, a museum for "problems of German history".

In the foreground looms a red-brick ruin still waiting either to be demolished or reconstructed—the bombed-out shell of the Imperial Museum of Arts and Crafts, its walls adorned with 1890s mosaics depicting the creative genius of mankind. Bushes and small trees have taken root on what little is left of the roof. Not far away is a grey reminder of Hitler's dismal taste in architecture, the former Ministry of Propaganda, where Dr. Joseph Goebbels ran the world's most powerful public relations machine. This pompous, oppressively rectilinear building has had its face lifted and is now used for government offices of the German Democratic Republic, or Deutsche Demokratische Republik, known locally as the DDR and more generally as East Germany.

Between the ruined museum and the reconstructed ministry runs a wall, the likes of which might be seen at modern penitentiaries the world over. Averaging 12 feet in height, this is the neat, efficient-looking concrete barrier known as the "modern Wall" to distinguish it from its sloppy, breeze-block predecessor, hastily built in 1961, remnants of which may still be seen here and there along the frontier between East and West

In West Berlin's Tiergarten, a bronze statue of Otto von Bismarck faces the Winged Victory erected to celebrate foreign victories that led in 1871 to the unification of Germany, with Bismarck as its Chancellor and Berlin its capital. Today these symbols of defunct Empire are swarmed over by tourists who come to see the city that is divided by a wall of concrete.

Berlin. On the eastern side of the modern Wall runs a strip of open ground strewn with tank obstacles—no one is going to crash through this wall with a truck or an armoured car—and beyond that a wire-mesh fence of matching height. At intervals, concrete watch-towers spring from the ground like giant tulips. The two or three men in each tower, dressed in grey uniforms reminiscent of the old *Feldgrau* of the Wehrmacht, are constantly busy surveying the terrain through field glasses, like conscientious lifeguards at a particularly dangerous beach.

But the people, East or West, who work within range of that baleful scrutiny have long since grown indifferent to it. They go about their tasks oblivious of the guards, the guns, the Wall: after all, this is Berlin. Only tourists still come, by the busload, to stare at the sight. They pour out of the buses and clamber on to the wooden platforms that a thoughtful West Berlin government has erected at several points for the benefit of those who want to peer over the Wall. A neatly lettered sign cautions visitors that they do so at their own risk and sends a shiver of apprehension down their spines. Yet nothing happens: the towers and the guards with field glasses are a kind of solemn ritual, the Berlin equivalent of the changing of the guard at Buckingham Palace—except that the guns are loaded, and now and then some foolhardy young man is caught trying to climb the inner fence. They rarely get as far as the Wall itself.

The inhabitants of Berlin have had more than 30 years to learn to live with this schizoid state of affairs. It is the only "normalcy" they know. (I use the word advisedly, remembering that it was coined by President Harding for another preposterous era, the Prohibition years of American history.) I think it bespeaks a certain collective genius that the Berliners have not only grown accustomed to the division of their city but have even managed to thrive on it. The average West Berliner has a higher income than the average American, just as the average East Berliner is better off, economically, than any of his neighbours in the Soviet bloc. Both halves, at any rate, can congratulate themselves on having made a successful comeback from the days when the city lay in ruins and there was more rubble in Berlin than in all the other towns of Germany put together.

Not that I propose to measure the city's greatness in terms of marks and pfennigs (or Marx and Engels for that matter). Berlin's golden time was the heroic but threadbare age of *The Threepenny Opera* by Bertolt Brecht and Kurt Weill; of Josef von Sternberg's film *The Blue Angel*, with Marlene Dietrich, and of the Paul Hindemith-Oskar Kokoschka opera, *Murder, the Hope of Women*. In the Twenties, the whole world camped on its doorstep, to listen to music and watch the theatre, or to argue about art in Kurfürstendamm cafés. Then the Third Reich put an end to all that. When the smoke of war had cleared, the dismal verdict was that "Germany has become a ghetto for Germans". In recent years the pendulum has been swinging back again. Foreigners are once more flocking to Berlin to live,

In a poignant reminder of what it means to live in a divided city, a woman at an East Berlin railway station holds aloft an umbrella tied with a scarf so that long absent relatives from the West will be sure to recognize her. After tensions between the two Berlins abated in the early 1970s, many West Berliners visited the East for the first time in 10 years or more.

as they did in the days of W. H. Auden and Christopher Isherwood, not because their governments have sent them but because they love the life.

One English writer who has lived in Berlin for several years speaks of the "tension in the air that keeps me on my toes". He loves to see the East-West yin-yang in action, even at home on his television set—Russian and Hungarian movies on the two DDR channels, along with more conventional fare on three or four Western channels. A young, romantically inclined South American composer I know says that he lives here "for the decadence, the absurdity, the music, and the opportunity to meet wonderfully argumentative yet co-operative girls".

People have tried to sum up the charms of the place with the phrase *Berliner Luft*—the air of Berlin. It is intended as a metaphor, I suppose, although one local scientist insists that Berlin air really does have a heady, champagne-like effect on the human constitution. More sober observers talk about "the quality of life", by which they mean that you can go to a different play or an opera every night of the week and—equally important —you can always find a parking space if you want to drive there. Berlin, unbelievable as it sounds, has virtually no traffic problem. Thanks to its very isolation deep within East Germany, the Western half of the city still has a humane ratio of cars to people, and in the Eastern half, where many consumer items remain in short supply, the cars are even fewer.

Certainly in West Berlin the *Berliner Luft* is also very much a matter of intangibles, compounded of the way people whistle in the streets, their incessant joke-telling and the charming insults they are always ready to heap on one another's heads. A prominent member of the American colony here confesses that, like me, he loves *Berlinerisch*—the amazing patois with which the locals murder conventional High German, and which falls on our prejudiced ears with the sound of angels' tongues. He learned it as a teenager before the war when his father, an American correspondent, sent him to a Berlin school. Afterwards he came back as an emissary of the U.S. government, found himself enamoured of the place and decided to stay on even when his appointment expired, although this meant resigning from the diplomatic service.

My own affection for Berlin is rooted in somewhat more ambivalent circumstances. I am not fond of Berlin beer, and am disinclined to spend much time in the Berlin pubs—*Kneipen*, or *Stampen* in local argot—where the heart of the city is said to beat. Hence I am condemned to remain a hopeless outsider for the rest of my life. Still, I return here with suspicious regularity to find out how the old town is getting on. It must be love.

I have come to Berlin many times from many directions, by train and plane as well as by car. But it was my mother who brought me the first time. I had been conceived in Montreux, on the Lake of Geneva, but she gave birth to me in Berlin, just in time to let me experience something of the city before it was devastated by Nazi ambition, American bombs and Russian artillery. My pre-war Berlin memories are those of a boy of six, seven, eight, nine—too young, you may think, to remember much about it, and yet not too young to have had the run of the city and to have acquired certain very clear and lasting insights about the place.

My Berlin was a spacious, dignified, beautiful city in the throes of being taken over by a gang of cut-throat vulgarians. It was perfectly plain to me (especially since I had frequent opportunity to compare their behaviour with that of the Swiss) that these unpleasant people with their brown and black shirts, their pistols and decorative daggers dangling from their belts, were wretched little men who dealt in fear. In pre-war Berlin vast numbers of these bully boys were for ever strutting about the streets trying to look important. They impressed one another with the same terrible zeal for obedience and *Ordnung* that I have since witnessed among the policemen and *Apparatchiks* of East Berlin.

We lived, my two sisters and I, an embarrassingly sheltered life on diplomat's row, in the Tiergartenstrasse, opposite the immense park that had once been a royal game preserve. Our house stood between the Dutch embassy and the Papal Nuncio's residence. I still remember the stern-faced gentlemen in black who used to watch from the windows when we made a noise in the garden: among them was the Vatican Secretary of State, Cardinal Pacelli, who had spent nine years in Berlin and was to become better known to history as Pope Pius XII.

In the park across the street there were bridle paths, a small lake full of wild ducks, a meandering stream, and something called the Sieges-Allee—the Victory Mall—that led to the tower of the Winged Victory. Here, in splendid array, stood the marble effigies of Germany's conquering heroes of the past—kings, emperors, princes and generals. A marble bench had been provided with each *Sieger* or victor so that one could sit and gaze to one's heart's content at the plumed helmets and coats of mail that the sculptors had rendered in meticulous detail. The warrior who made the deepest impression on me was *Otto mit dem Pfeil* (Otto with the Arrow), who had been obliged, my governess told me, to live the last years of his life with the point of an arrow embedded in his skull. The sculptor, as I recall, had depicted him holding his helmet under his arm, his poor head swathed in bandages.

The row of victors had been sculpted before the First World War (after the Second they were given a decent burial among the rubble). There were no *Sieger* from the First World War, of course, although elsewhere the heroic memory of the losers of 1914-18 was constantly being evoked—in memorials, radio programmes, films, posters, veterans' appeals. My own young feelings in the matter were rather mixed. I knew that my father had enlisted in the Prussian cavalry at the start of the war. We had a photograph of him at the age of 18—a slender youth on a very large horse—

Two West Berliners fly a kite near a U.S. radar installation sited on top of the Teufelsberg, or Devil's Mountain. At 377 feet, the "mountain" is the highest of three giant mounds created from wartime rubble. Its slopes include public gardens as well as two ski jumps and a toboggan run supplied with artificial snow.

setting out for Russia with a spiked helmet and an enormous sabre. (It occurs to me now that Franz Kafka would have looked like that had he been able to pass the physical.)

But after a year and a half at the front it had taken my father two years in military hospitals to recover from assorted fevers. Understandably, he never told us tales of derring-do under shot and shell, such as were to be heard daily on the radio. Instead, if the war was mentioned at all, my mother always brought up the painful subject of her cousin Raymond, on the British side of the family, who had been killed fighting the Germans at Ypres. He had been the only son, and neither his womenfolk nor mine ever recovered from the shock: his four sisters, indeed, had all remained unmarried and taken up Good Works among the London Poor.

I harboured a secret admiration for the Prussian cavalry, however, because I used to watch the old Field Marshal von Mackensen trotting by on his morning ride through the Tiergarten. He was well over 80 at the

Two Cities in One

Berlin, 110 miles inside East Germany, is divided by the Wall (brown), whose 28½-mile length is plotted in full on the inset map below. It joins the so-called "country" Wall (tan), also shown on the inset map. This runs along West Berlin's western boundary, sealing the city off from the East German countryside (grey). Luckily West Berlin has plenty of farmland as well as extensive parks and forests (light green) on either side of the River Havel. Like East Berlin, the West is also generously provided with lakes and waterways (blue).

The major buildings, monuments, streets and squares in the inner districts of East (pink) and West (dark green) Berlin are designated on the large map. Most of the historic monuments are in the East, which contains the old capital's city centre, or *Mitte*.

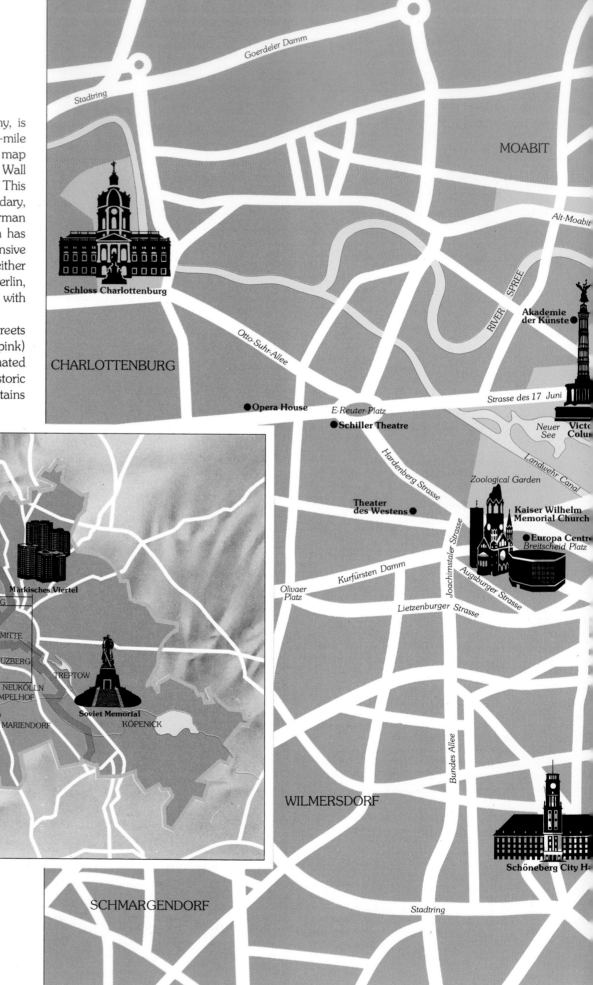

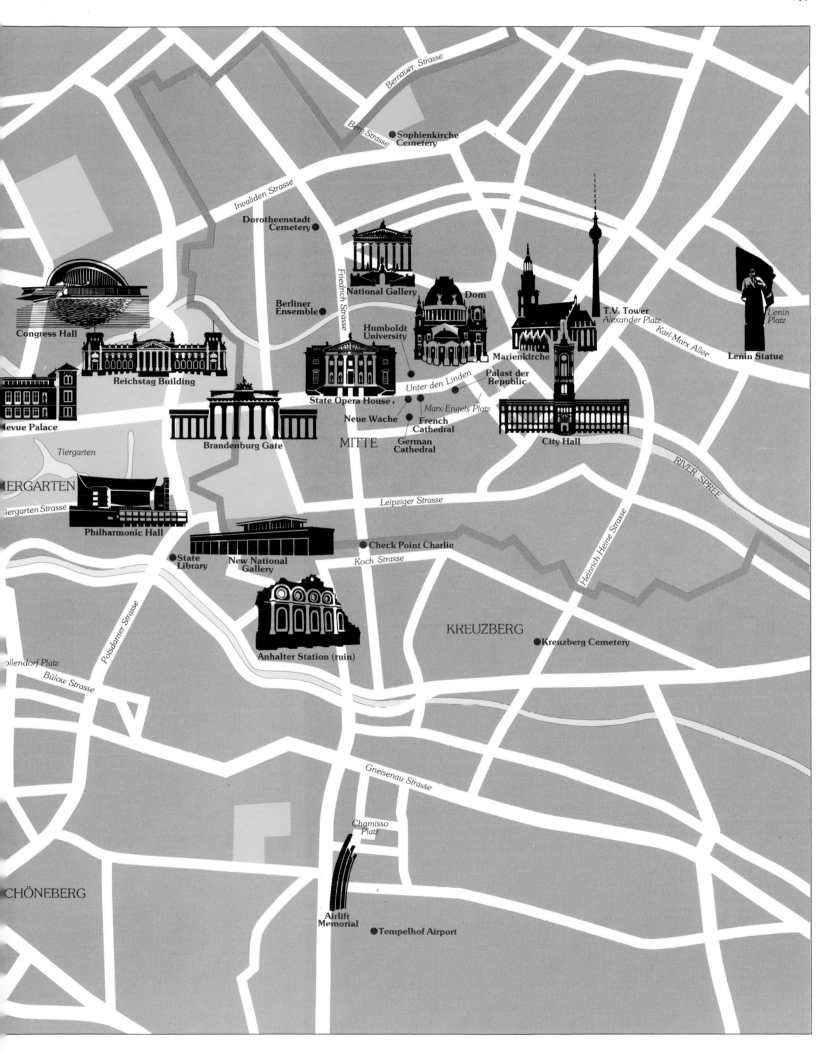

Bernauer Strasse

Berg Strasse

Sophienkirche
Cemetery

Invaliden Strasse

Dorotheenstadt
Cemetery

T.V. Tower
Alexander Platz

Lenin
Platz

Congress Hall

National Gallery

Dom

Lenin Statue

Berliner
Ensemble

Friedrich Strasse

Humboldt
University

Reichstag Building

Marienkirche

Kari-Marx Allee

Revue Palace

Unter den Linden

Palast der
Republic

State Opera House

Marx-Engels Platz

Brandenburg Gate

Neue Wache

French
Cathedral

City Hall

MITTE

German
Cathedral

Tiergarten

RIVER SPREE

TIERGARTEN

Tiergarten Strasse

Leipziger Strasse

Philharmonic Hall

Heinrich-Heine Strasse

State
Library

New National
Gallery

Check Point Charlie

Koch Strasse

Potsdamer Strasse

KREUZBERG

Kreuzberg Cemetery

ollendorf Platz

Bülow Strasse

Anhalter Station (ruin)

Gneisenau Strasse

Chamisso
Platz

SCHÖNEBERG

Airlift
Memorial

Tempelhof Airport

time, and always wore mufti. But there was no doubting that this was a cavalryman of the old school, silver-haired, straight as a ramrod; a survivor from the age of the *Sieger*.

In the Berlin of those days von Mackensen must have been the only one entitled to a uniform who was not wearing one. After Hitler became German Chancellor in 1933 the city suddenly blossomed out in a wide variety of uniforms: not only the army in grey and the navy in blue but, far more numerous and assorted, the members of Nazi organizations. There were Stormtroopers in brown; SS men in black; the Reichsarbeitsdienst (labour corps) in a sort of ochre; the National Socialist Kraftfahrerkorps (for drivers of cars) in black; the Hitler Youth in shorts, brown shirts and Sam Browne belts; girls of the BDM (League of German Girls) in black skirts and white blouses; even the six-year-old *Pimpfe*, or cub scouts of the Nazi movement, dressed in black as mini-SS men.

They swelled the cheering crowds that stood in front of the Reich Chancellery chanting, "We want to see our Führer!", the cheering crowds that lined the avenues for the triumphal reception of Benito Mussolini, the cheering crowds that celebrated the "700th birthday of Berlin"—an anniversary that, I learn to my belated surprise, was based on a conveniently fictitious date.

Yet, in spite of the proliferating uniforms and the public hysteria, I recall that there were astonishing numbers of ordinary Berliners who resisted the blandishments of Dr. Goebbels' propaganda. Even on those rare occasions when the Nazis were out of uniform, one could still tell them from the non-Nazis by the way they spoke: the Nazis always barked, as though they were already in a war, giving orders to subordinates. The decent people spoke softly and tended to wear worried expressions—rightly so, as it turned out. "*Kooft euch Kämme*," they used to say to each other. "*Et komm'n lausije Zeiten.*" (You'd better stock up on combs; lousy times are coming.)

Berlin then had more outdoor monuments and statues than Rome, just as it had more bridges than Venice (a statistic that still startles visitors). Directly across the street from our house stood a statue of Theodor Fontane, the "German Flaubert" whose novels and essays describe Berlin in its 19th-Century heyday. When we packed up and left, first for England and then the United States, I was just tall enough to reach Fontane's marble boots if I stood on tiptoe. When I returned to Berlin for the first time in the 1950s, I walked over to our old address and found that the entire block had been bombed into rubble during the war. Now there was grass and shrubbery on both sides of the street. Only the statue of Fontane was still standing there, untouched by the bombs, although looking neglected and forlorn in that abandoned corner of the park. And to my surprise he seemed to have shrunk in size; now, without stretching, I was able to touch the marble folds of his frock coat!

Flanked on one side by the U-Bahn, West Berlin's underground railway, and on the other by a road, the Landwehr Canal winds through the city. The canal, now popular with anglers and boatmen, is part of a 114-mile system of waterways that carried much of Berlin's trade during the city's growth in the 19th Century.

Decorative medallions set into the railings of a bridge leading to the 16th-Century Citadel of Spandau in outer West Berlin constitute a capsule history of German militarism. Each represents the headgear of a particular era, from the face-protecting iron helms of medieval knights to the more familiar profile of the helmet worn by soldiers of the Wehrmacht.

Helm, late 13th Century

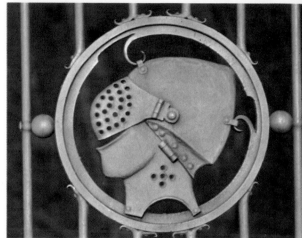

Armet, c. 1440

Kettle hat, c. 1450

Cavalry helmet, mid-17th Century

Berlin, meanwhile, had been flattened and had made a new start. Physically the city was in ruins; psychologically it was already well on the way to recovery. People no longer barked at one another; their souls had been scrubbed clean by misery. Even policemen smiled. Next to London and Amsterdam, Berlin had become the most tolerant city in Europe—at least in the Western sectors. In the East it was another story. Most of the DDR policemen and party functionaries with whom I came into contact were busy upholding the best traditions of that German officialdom whose devotion to duty and sense of rectitude have always made life miserable for everybody else. The boots of the Volkspolizei, the so-called People's Police, were not as shiny as I had remembered those of the Nazis, but their tread was as heavy and the atmosphere in that half of the city nearly as oppressive as before.

This psychological division of the city into palpably "tense" and visibly "relaxed" halves reflected the convolutions of post-war international politics and Berlin's uncomfortably exposed position on the strategic chessboard. At Yalta in 1945 it had seemed reasonable enough for Churchill, Roosevelt and Stalin to agree on a joint military occupation of the city: it was assumed that the Allies would pursue a common policy towards their defeated foe. Instead, differences between East and West soon escalated into the Cold War and the line between their respective armies of occupation in Germany froze into a hostile frontier. The Western half, protected by American military might and sustained economically by the Marshall Plan, became a "Federal Republic" faintly suggestive of a United States of Germany. The Eastern half, under Soviet tutelage, was duly transformed into a "Democratic Republic" along Stalinist lines, with East Berlin as its capital.

Had Berlin been located on the frontier between these two rivals, some sort of condominium might have been arranged. But the city lies deep within the DDR, only some 40 miles from the Polish border. The American, French and British sectors, with roughly two million of the city's three million people, form an enclave without a corridor; the nearest West German point on the autobahn lies at Helmstedt, more than 100 miles away, a circumstance from which most of Berlin's post-war troubles stem. As a consequence, truncated Berlin is not only a capital without a real country but also an industrial centre without free and direct access to a hinterland in which to sell its produce and recruit its workers.

In 1948 the Soviets put the viability of this enclave to the test by cutting its surface links to the West and turning off the electricity. A hastily improvised U.S. and British airlift proved what no one had suspected until then—that a city of more than two million can be supplied entirely by air if necessary. Moreover, 11 months of siege and psychological warfare stiffened the backbone of the West Berliners. The Western Allies had shown their

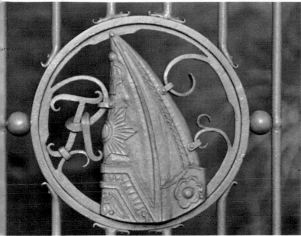

nadier's cap, c. 1800

kelhaube, c. 1880

ko, c. 1890

rmacht steel helmet

determination to defend their occupation rights in the city. Perhaps more importantly, the West Berliners themselves had demonstrated their willingness and ability to exist as an anomaly, an island-state in the middle of a continent. Henceforth they called themselves, with justifiable pride, *Die Insulaner*, The Islanders.

A city of more conventional size and aspect might well have succumbed to the blockade. But here a historical accident served to tip the scales. The town planners who drew the city limits of modern Berlin in 1920 were unusually generous and included not only the existing suburbs but also many of the outlying farm communities. With 346 square miles, Berlin was intended to rival London as the most widespread city in Europe. Even after it was divided, with eight Eastern districts going to the Soviet sector, the remaining 12 districts (with 54 per cent of the land) still covered twice as much ground as either Frankfurt or Stuttgart.

If Paris were to be cut in half and isolated the same way, people in the enclave *arrondissements* would soon be climbing up the walls with claustrophobia. West Berlin, with its 25,000 acres of canals, rivers, lakes, farmland, parks, and forests—the Grunewald, with its $15\frac{1}{2}$ square miles of pine and deciduous trees, is the largest forest within city limits anywhere in the world—had sufficient breathing space, not to say *Lebensraum*, to withstand the psychological pressures of a long siege.

In recent years, thanks to the agreements reached in 1971 between the Soviet Union, the United States, Britain and France, it has been much easier for West Berliners to visit relatives in the East or to take an occasional holiday in the DDR. Yet at no time has either side been happy with the division. The DDR authorities, understandably, have always regarded West Berlin as a thorn in their side. No other country in the world has to put up with a foreign enclave in its capital city: Gibraltar, Hong Kong, Monaco, Liechtenstein and Andorra are all on the periphery of the countries from which they have been carved. Could one imagine a London in which an area from Mayfair to Kensington belongs to Albania? No wonder Berlin suffers from a peculiar form of siege mentality in which both sides feel beleaguered—the East ideologically, the West territorially.

During the 1960s, as cultural correspondent for a U.S. magazine, I returned often to Berlin—East and West—to cover the post-war theatrical and operatic resurgence. At the time, the Western half was undergoing an identity crisis, searching for a role to play in the post-war world. Economically it was back on its feet. New buildings were springing up everywhere, factories were humming, people who had been content merely to have got off alive suddenly found themselves more prosperous than ever before. Even the political situation had been stabilized, after a fashion, when in 1961 the East Germans erected the Wall and put an end to the wholesale exodus of their labour force. The West Berliners, however, wanted something more for their city than just a carbon copy of the general West German "economic miracle"—the celebrated *Wirtschaftswunder*. Berlin had once been the capital of an empire; if now it could not be the capital of a country, it ought at least to function as a cultural centre.

Perhaps I should explain that *Kultur* in Germany is not the haphazard and largely private affair it tends to be in Paris, London or New York. The arts have always been taken very seriously by German governments, whether monarchist or republican. The tradition of state-sponsored culture—of *Kulturpolitik* (a very German concept, this)—goes back to the days when Germany was a patchwork of independent duchies and principalities, and every court worthy of the name supported its own theatre and opera house, as well as a household staff of musicians, poets and painters. J. S. Bach held a series of state appointments; Goethe served as minister to a duke; Richard Wagner nearly bankrupted the King of Bavaria; even 20th-Century mavericks like Paul Klee and Bertolt Brecht drew government pay cheques in one capacity or another.

Berlin's cultural renaissance, therefore, was deemed to be essentially a government affair. If New York wants to build a Lincoln Center, its sponsors are obliged to go hat in hand to the city's millionaire art patrons; in Germany, theatres and opera houses are built with public funds and kept going by generous annual subsidies. No one objects if the theatre loses money with every ticket sold; culture is not expected to be self-supporting—but then, neither are armies. Moreover, an employee of a state theatre is not, as on Broadway or in London's West End, a freelance artist who must expect to live from season to season and hand to mouth; he is a civil servant who enjoys that greatest of desiderata, *eine gesicherte Stellung*, a permanent position, as secure as a job in the post office.

There has always been room here and there, of course, for a poet starving in a garret or a painter without a professorship. But traditionally it is the public institutions that have set the pace, especially in the city that wanted to rival Athens, and had built its theatres and museums to look just like Greek temples. Berlin, indeed, has long been known by the symphony orchestra, the art galleries and the opera company it keeps.

As the *Wunder* gathered momentum and the government subsidies began to pour in, West Berlin became a hotbed of cultural activity. The inauguration of the new West Berlin Opera House in 1961 marked, in the words of the then mayor, Willy Brandt, "a big step towards making Berlin the centre of Germany". It was followed by a splendid Philharmonic Hall with an auditorium in the shape of a figure-eight, a new Academy of Arts, a new National Library and a new National Gallery designed by the exiled Berlin architect Mies van der Rohe, whose best-known buildings stand in New York and Chicago. The theatre also proceeded to flourish mightily in both halves of the city. On any given night of the season you could have your choice of performances in more than a dozen theatres in the West

This sketch of an entwined couple on a dance floor provides an example of the earthy humour in the works of Heinrich Zille (1858-1929). His cartoons of Berlin working-class life are still immensely popular and nowadays are found hanging in galleries and public places such as the restaurant at right in West Berlin.

and up to 10 theatres in the East, as well as several concerts and three first-rate operatic performances—two in the East, one in the West.

More than 30 years had passed since the Golden Twenties, but people in Berlin still remembered that legendary epoch when, as the publisher Walter Kahnert once told me, "You'd go to a café and at the next table you'd see the world's greatest opera singer, and over there the greatest poet, the foremost actor, the best novelist. We *were* an Athens; a city of the arts almost too glorious to describe. We used to stay up and talk all night, every night."

Post-war Berlin could not hope to regain that lost paradise, but at least it could build on the little that remained. Many of the famous exiles were lured back from abroad, some for only a short time, others permanently. The stage director Carl Ebert, for example (one of the founders of the Glyndebourne Festival in Britain), returned from California to reorganize the new German Opera—successor to the same company that he had directed in the early Thirties. Paul Hindemith came to conduct, Fritz Lang and Leopold Lindtberg to direct, Elisabeth Bergner to act. In 1964 Erwin Piscator, another great director who came home to roost, created the greatest scandal of his career by staging a première of Rolf Hochhuth's *Der Stellvertreter (The Representative)*, a controversial play about Pope Pius XII and his dealings with the Nazis.

I also recall the première of the German version of *My Fair Lady*: the heroine, still a poor flower-seller from one of the shabbier parts of town, can express herself only in Berlin gutter-argot; but after learning to speak in the clipped accents of proper High German, she manages to pass for a Hungarian Princess. This plot variation rather puzzled the Berliners, who had never associated their native dialect with class distinctions: even the Kaiser, after all, took great pride in speaking *Berlinerisch*.

In the East there was the Berliner Ensemble, a formidable company directed until his death in 1956 by Brecht, the foremost German play-wright of the 20th Century. The old State Opera in its Greek-revival building on Unter den Linden had been lovingly restored and, at the Comic Opera, the director Walter Felsenstein produced what was easily the liveliest lyric theatre on three continents. Thus in Berlin, at the focal point of the confict between East and West, the things that were being done during the 1950s and 1960s in the arts, in publishing and architecture made the city in Kahnert's words, "the most exciting place on earth".

So much was happening on the cultural scene that Berlin came to resemble a sort of three-ring circus of the arts. Fortunately, I had discovered an infallible guide and gossip-monger to help me keep abreast of the situation—the redoubtable Frau Schmidt (as I shall call her), who ran the *Pension* where I always stayed on my visits to the city.

When I first knew her, Frau Schmidt was a handsome blonde in her late fifties with an insatiable appetite for anything that took place on a stage.

One of the most avant-garde commercial buildings in pre-war Berlin was Grünfeld's department store, which was founded by the author's great-grandfather. The art deco structure, inaugurated in a blaze of neon in 1928, was a prominent example of the Bauhaus style that revolutionized German design in the 1920s. It was destroyed by bombing in 1945.

By the time she had reached her seventies, she no longer got out as often as she used to; but in her halcyon days she went to the theatre, or to a concert or the opera at least four or five evenings a week. Sometimes, when one of her lodgers was in the cast, she would also spend an afternoon at a dress rehearsal.

Frau Schmidt was as statuesque as any of the Wagnerian Valkyries she liked to hear at the opera, but her favourite work, curiously enough, was Gluck's fragile *Orpheus et Eurydice* which, by a quirk of her Berlin dialect, she always pronounced as though she were saying *Orpheus und Eure Dicke* (Orpheus and Your Fat Lady). That seemed to describe the situation perfectly. Frau Schmidt's wholehearted devotion to Orpheus made her a kind of vestal matron, and with the years she had become a connoisseur of considerable note. She knew who all the singers were, not only in Berlin but in any other opera house of consequence; what they had sung, and what they could sing. She had a mind like a steel filing cabinet when it came to singers, actors, actresses and directors, and she would always tell me who had slept with whom.

In the musical department she had a sixth sense about which of the dozen pianists or violinists making a Berlin debut that season was destined to be the sensation of the year, and she always had a fifth-row seat for the occasion. I never knew her to be wrong. She recognized greatness in performers the world then knew little about, yet I doubt whether she ever had time or inclination to read anything more than a programme note.

Frau Schmidt was not the widow of an opera star, as one might have expected; she was an authentic member of the Berlin working class. She began her career as a chamber-maid in one of the city's better hotels, and worked her way up to *Inspectrice* of the housekeeping staff. At the end of

At West Berlin's Nollendorfplatz station a stage coach sits across the disused tracks to the East, advertising a flea market held in old railway carriages.

the Second World War she found herself jobless (the hotel had been hit by a bomb) and with a fatherless child on her hands (her boyfriend had been killed at Stalingrad).

Nothing daunted, she rented a derelict 14-room apartment near the centre of West Berlin, not far from the Kurfürstendamm, and turned it into a *Pension*. There was a desperate shortage of hotel rooms at the time and her beds were always filled—preferably, of course, with actors and musicians, who could usually be found talking shop around her huge dining-room table. Later, after the hotel shortage eased, many of them continued to prefer Frau Schmidt's to the Hilton. It was rather like living in a conservatory, what with the gargling and voice-stretching exercises that issued from the rooms in the morning.

The *Pension Schmidt* occupied the fourth floor of one wing of an apartment building whose architecture would be called late Victorian in England; here the style, still common in Berlin, is known as Wilhelmine (in honour of Kaisers Wilhelm I and Wilhelm II) or *Gründerzeit*, i.e. the "time of the founders" (of commercial enterprises). The rooms, like so many I remember from my childhood, had enormously high ceilings with ornate plaster mouldings, high, double-glazed bay windows, floors of polished parquet covered with Persian carpets and brass door handles in the shape of Chinese dragons. Her bathrooms provided the ideal acoustic environment for vocal exercises. Floral tiles ran from floor to ceiling, and there was a king-sized tub on lion feet, flanked by a wickerwork bath chair and a shelf holding four varieties of bath salts. The toilets were tucked into narrow chambers of their own—up to 20 feet long but only four feet wide.

Frau Schmidt did not call them toilets. She referred to them by the classic euphemism, *Wo der Kaiser zu Fuss geht* (Where the Emperor betakes himself on foot). The walls of the *Pension* were covered with oils, sketches and watercolours which she had, in weak moments, accepted in lieu of rent from a layabout lodger who spent six months of the year painting in Ibiza, the rest scrounging from Frau Schmidt.

Breakfast was the only meal served at the *Pension*. Since Frau Schmidt liked to eat, she expected her guests to eat as much as she did, insisting that they work their way through a proper German breakfast consisting of coffee and rolls, butter, marmalade, soft-boiled eggs, cheese and sliced sausage. This typical groaning board seemed to be a form of overcompensation for the lean years of the war. She rarely missed a chance to berate the Nazis for having caused the death of her man and the demise of her city. Still, something of their dubious philosophy may have rubbed off on her thinking, as it has on many of the people who had to spend 12 years listening to Dr. Goebbels' propaganda. When her son, a dentist, married a girl whose mother was Polish, Frau Schmidt told me, in the same critical tone that she reserved for tenors who sang flat: "Her legs are very short. *Das ist keine edle Rasse!*" (That is not a noble race!)

Going to the opera with Frau Schmidt was a privilege she accorded only to the *cognoscenti* among her guests. The ushers treated her as if she were the Begum Aga Khan and, during the intermission, she would meet several like-minded ladies of great probity and wit with whom, in rapier-like thrusts of the Berlin vernacular, she would dissect the evening's performance. When she applauded, the sound rang through the theatre like thunderclaps; but if something failed to meet with her approval, her silence was ominous and fierce. Afterwards we would repair to a café on the Kurfürstendamm for a final reassessment of the evening, spiced with the latest operatic gossip, while we demolished vast slices of chocolate cake topped with the obligatory mountain of whipped cream.

"Frau Schmidt is the reason I like to perform in Berlin," an actor from Frankfurt once told me at the breakfast table. "There are dozens of good theatre towns in Germany, but it's here that audiences are knowledgeable and intense. You can feel them leaning into a play; it's an electrical current running through the theatre. It does wonders for your acting to know that they care about what you do. They even applaud in the right places. I don't know any other audiences like them."

I myself think of Frau Schmidt as having given not only the theatre but the entire city its reason for existence. She and her *Pension* still strike me as the closest thing to a living tradition that Berlin happens to possess. For this city, more than any other I have known, has memories and a history, but no real sense of continuity with the past. For more than 30 years everything in Berlin has had to be improvised, even such basic considerations as the legal status of the city.

Other communities are sustained by a nexus of symbols and traditions that have been built up over the years, sometimes for centuries. One thinks of the State Opening of Parliament at Westminster, the Garde Republicaine clattering across the Place de la Concorde, the Pope blessing the crowds in St. Peter's Square, the St. Patrick's Day parade moving along New York's Fifth Avenue. But Berlin has no Trooping the Colour, no be-wigged judges, no medieval guildhalls, not even a proper "Four Hundred" to fulfil the usual functions of a social élite. Even the trees in the Tiergarten and Grunewald are a post-war generation, planted to replace those cut down during the war. I can recognize the remaining landmarks of the Berlin I knew as a child, but its psychological profile is utterly new and alien to me. There were never any real precedents for a city like this one—a house divided against itself that does somehow manage to stand. The decisions that have enabled it to survive are often makeshift and tentative. In spite of the skill of the town planners and the solidity of the architecture, most of what has happened here since 1945—the "Year Zero"— has an ad hoc quality about it.

Yet, by the same token, Berlin's very insecurity helps to make it "the most exciting place on earth". It is an ongoing experiment, combining

A young West Berliner unwinds with a Weisse mit Schuss, a beer and raspberry concoction, in one of the crowded street cafés that line the Kurfürstendamm. A mecca for writers and artists in the 1920s, the Ku-damm, as it is affectionately called, is now a busy boulevard that rivals the best in Paris or Rome.

elements of hope and fear, fulfilment and frustration. At least, people here are not committed to their parents' vision of the future: surely it is just as well that they buried the *Sieger* in the rubble of yesterday's Victory Mall.

Problems are solved as they arise, and the solutions are often remarkably original and humane. For example, when the Wall went up, several West Berlin elevated stations belonging to an East Berlin division of the transit system were cut off and taken out of service. One of them is at the Nollendorfplatz, a square near the main business district of West Berlin. Rather than allow a useful piece of real estate to rot away, the West Berlin Senate moved two strings of ancient subway cars into the deserted station and rented them out to dealers of stamps, coins and assorted junk. Today the Nollendorfplatz is the city's busiest flea market.

Something of the same ingenuity marks the arrangements that have been made between the two halves of the city on many "non-political" issues. Actually, both sides are convinced that there is no such thing as a non-political issue, but are prepared to concede that some are less political than others. In any case, East and West are aware that, however stringently the division of the city might be enforced, in certain vital matters such as air pollution control, Spree River navigation and so on, the two halves are locked in eternal embrace, like the sinning lovers in Dante's circle of sighs. Hence their willingness to reach a compromise.

Most of West Berlin's sewage, for example, has always been pumped to sewage farms and treatment plants in East Berlin and the DDR. The West pays for this service, of course. Even in the darkest days of the blockade, no one ever threatened to block the sewage pipes leading to the East, for that would cause the sewage to flow into rivers and canals that are also used by the East for water supply. Most of West Berlin's rubbish is also dumped on DDR territory—for a fee. The municipal rubbish trucks make their daily runs through a heavily guarded gate in the Wall, then over a special access road lined with high wire fences to what must be the world's most heavily fortified rubbish dump. There is not the remotest chance of their picking up anyone on the empty trip out.

Under these circumstances, the average Berliner has seen just about every kind of political and territorial absurdity and has developed an imperturbable *sang-froid* that would do credit to an English colonel. The West Berlin U-Bahn (Underground) provides another typical example. Two of its lines actually tunnel beneath and traverse the East Berlin "bulge". One of them makes no stops at all in the East, where all of its six erstwhile stations were sealed off when the Wall went up. The other— Line 6, connecting Alt-Mariendorf in the south with Tegel in the north— runs under the Wall to the Friedrichstrasse station, where it makes one stop before re-entering West Berlin.

Every day thousands of people commute to work this way, in both directions, passing 20 feet or so beneath the most lethal frontier in the world. The doors open at the Friedrichstrasse: people with appropriate papers get off here to pass through the passport and customs control into the East. Needless to say, East Berliners (with a few rare exceptions) are not permitted to get on. Upstairs the exits are patrolled by border guards with dogs and machine pistols. Downstairs, the West Berlin commuters on the packed train scarcely look up from their newspapers as the doors close and the train moves off. This could be Charing Cross station instead of the cellars of the East German state police.

"Berlin is a great arena of competitive life-styles," says a local newspaperman with a wry smile. "We may be a testing ground for the Utopia of the 21st Century. It's just that the machinery still needs a little adjusting." Without the incessant ideological competition, I suspect, Berlin might have quietly subsided into being just another East European capital, a sort of Bucharest on the Spree.

Part of the excitement, certainly, derives from the cloak-and-dagger stuff that still goes on year after year—the rival agents, "spooks", infiltrators, eavesdroppers and provocateurs whose activities constitute one of the most remunerative of the local cottage industries. You will not find them listed in the telephone book, but I am reliably informed that they carry on quietly under various discreet and ingenious façades: the "Council for World Peace and Artificial Insemination", let's say, or the "Global Society of Comparative Embryology".

In Berlin, if the "Institute for the Study of Integrational Dynamics" invites you to a cocktail party, you may expect to find an electronic bug in your martini. As for the nice, grey-haired gentleman who converses so knowledgeably about Egyptian archaeology, is it really Colonel Creighton of the Topographic Survey, or Comrade Ivanov of Outer Mongolian Intelligence? Conversation between two little girls, overheard in the well-stocked shopping centre of one of West Berlin's American military compounds: "My father's a spook! Is your father a spook, too?"

Of course, I may be doing the rival espionage outfits an injustice; to an imagination schooled on Eric Ambler and John Le Carré every innocent organization with a villa in the Grunewald can take on a slightly sinister hue. Nevertheless, I have been told by an unimpeachable source that both sides employ several thousands of "specialists", although I am at a loss to imagine what secrets they could possibly be attempting to filch. The really important decisions affecting Berlin are made in Washington and Moscow. It probably has something to do with Parkinson's law of boondoggling: the "intelligence communities" have been here so long they are reluctant to let go of a good thing. It is a pleasant, sunny spot for skulduggery, with plenty of parking space and a good selection of first-run feature films. In the old days there were certain hazards. Agents would kidnap their rivals with a fair degree of regularity, and double agents were known to disappear without trace. But the "funeral in Berlin" has gone out of style. The first and second generations of operatives have come in from the cold and written their (expurgated) memoirs.

Spying nowadays is done with an assortment of sophisticated electronic devices that would have Dr. No gnashing his buck teeth in envy. "Our men don't have to bestir themselves any more," my well-informed friend observed. "They don't like to leave the sanctuary of their country club; field work isn't their line." Still, on the whole he regards it as a fair exchange. "We take in their rubbish on our monitoring stations; they take in ours by dump truck."

Although the Cold War has abated, *Berliner Luft* continues to have a bracing effect that derives from the city's position astride the fault-line of power politics. "The very frictions of the place keep us thinking about the world and what we want done with it," explains a West Berlin university instructor who came here from one of the towns in the Rhineland. "People in the Federal Republic talk about their cars and houses, and how well off they are. In Berlin they talk about art and politics. They express their opinions, they argue with one another, they're alive."

Indeed, passions still run high in the theatres, the cafés, the universities. To add fuel to the arguments there are the constant contrasts and contradictions that are possible only in this political landscape where a visitor from the outside, at least, can partake of both possible worlds: the Schiller Theatre and the Berliner Ensemble; the Philharmonic Orchestra and the State Opera; the New Eden strip club and the Festival of Political Songs.

"Sometimes I have the uncomfortable feeling that the whole damned show is being put on for my benefit," Frau Schmidt said. "Well I think it's a lovely town. I won't leave here unless they throw me out. And even then I'd only go on the last train from Berlin."

The Great Wall of Germany

An East German border guard telephones a report from his watch-tower as a comrade scans the Western side of the Wall, keeping an eye on all movements.

The barrier that divides Berlin is much more forbidding than the simple term "the Wall" implies. The 15-foot-high concrete barricade itself is only one of the formidable obstacles that form a grim death zone up to 300 yards deep along West Berlin's 99½-mile boundary. There are dog runs, tank traps, flares set off by concealed trip wires, fences rigged with listening devices and alarms, see-in-the-dark television cameras monitored by guards in machine-gun towers and open stretches of ground seeded with vicious fragmentation mines. Each successful escape from East Germany is carefully analysed in order to find new deterrents, which are then tested against the skills of special escape experts before being installed. And yet, in spite of these brutally effective precautions, a few people each year risk making the run for freedom.

This photograph, taken from a window in the West, provides a rare cross-view of the lethal obstacle course that divides Berlin. The woman and child walking along an East Berlin street (left side of picture) are separated from West Berlin by a high fence, a patrolled road, another fence, tank traps, mined ground 30 yards wide and finally (upper right) the concrete Wall, whitewashed to silhouette any escapee lucky enough to have got that far.

A stony-faced East German guard mans the Wall at a spot where it blocks a street still marked with a sign erected when it was an uninterrupted thoroughfare.

Constant Surveillance

The duties of the young *Grepos*, East German border guards who man the Wall, are doubly unpleasant. Not only must they be ready to kill their own countrymen, but they are also expected to watch their comrades—even photographing one another's movements. The regime has reason to be suspicious. In the first two months following the building of the Wall in 1961 some 150 guards fled to the West, and a few still escape each year.

A West Berliner, curious about repair work on part of the Wall, peers through the barrier at East German border guards while one of them takes his photograph.

Along the Bernauerstrasse, where an old stretch of the Wall (foreground) has been superseded by a new barrier (background), a church— ironically named the Church of Reconciliation— has been stranded in a no-man's land of patrol lanes and tank traps. On the Western side of the boundary (right foreground) has been painted the sub-title of an 18th-Century German play that has become a watchword against tyranny.

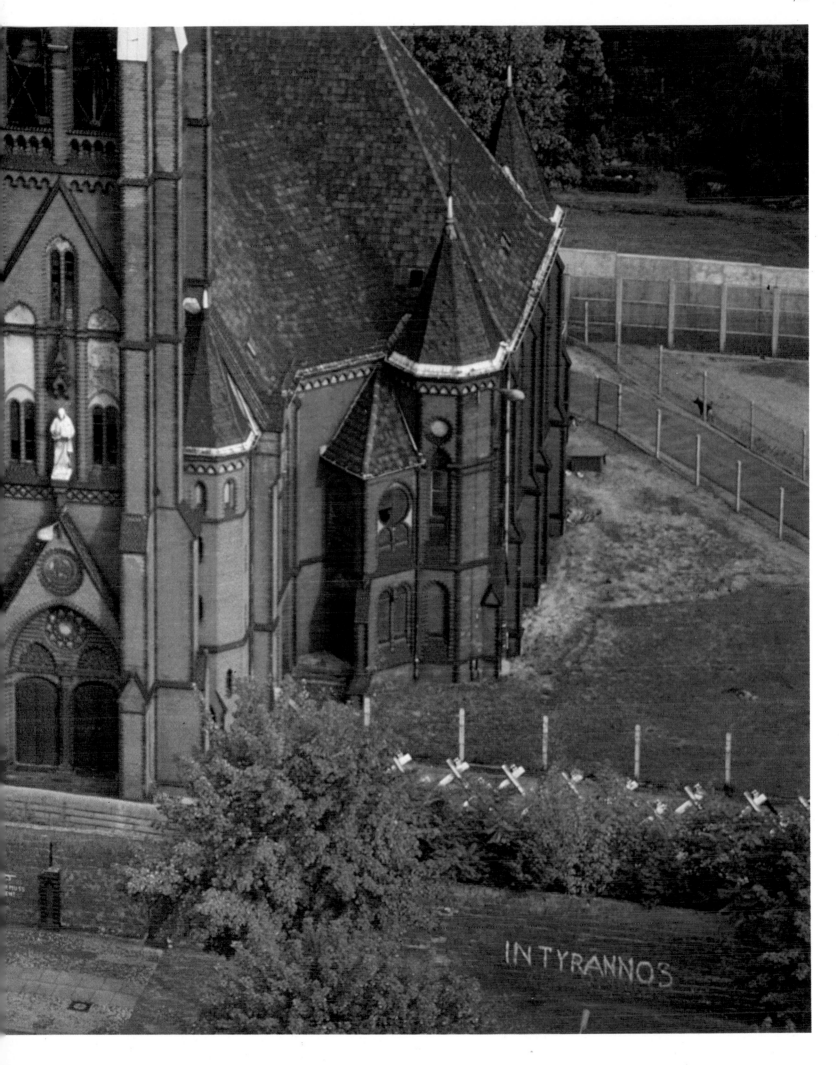

Fading photographs pinned to a wooden cross commemorate some of those killed in escape attempts.

Memorials to Those Who Died Trying

Before the Wall went up in 1961, the flow of refugees from East to West Berlin reached as much as 20,000 in a single day. Since then perhaps 25 a year have made it across the barrier and scores have died in the attempt, a bitter fact recorded by memorials in the West. As the Wall was made more daunting, some of those trapped behind it showed signs of strain, leading to a syndrome that one psychiatrist called *Mauerkrankheit*—"Wall sickness".

Den Toten der Mauer
13.8.1961 – 13.8.1971

Fresh wreaths adorn a shrine to those who fell during the first decade of the Wall's existence. It lies athwart an old tram-line blocked by concrete.

YOU ARE LEAVING
THE AMERICAN SECTOR
ВЫ ВЫЕЗЖАЕТЕ ИЗ
АМЕРИКАНСКОГО СЕКТОРА
VOUS SORTEZ
DU SECTEUR AMERICAIN
SIE VERLASSEN DEN AMERIKANISCHEN SEKTORS

DIE MAUER MU

"The Wall must go!" demand West Berlin Marxists whose hammer-sickle-and-rifle emblem symbolizes their opposition to both capitalism and "Stalinism".

But as the Wall passed its 15th anniversary in 1976, there was little hope of its being removed. Like the East German regime itself, the Wall has come to stay.

2

West of the Divide

On DDR maps of Berlin, the Western sectors of the city are shown as a ghastly blank—a sort of Empty Quarter, as they used to call part of Arabia. East Berliners are permitted to see how the streets run in their own boroughs, but beyond the Wall there is nothing but a grey, anonymous blob, as though the city had ceased to exist. Well, it's there—should there be any lingering doubt in anyone's mind. West Berlin on its own is the largest city in West Germany. It has nearly two-thirds of the population of Greater Berlin (more than two million people), slightly more than half the land area (185 square miles) and about 90 per cent of the *joie de vivre*.

It is no accident that so many of the foreign diplomats stationed in the East are for ever crossing over to the West, living the good life and relaxing from the rigours of the DDR. West Berlin, indeed, is a holiday camp compared to the disciplinarian East; it is a city of light whose glow by night can be seen for miles around. The contrast with the East was even more pronounced in the 1950s when the DDR still rationed its electricity. If you approached the city by car or train through the browned-out DDR, the lights of West Berlin on the horizon seemed to symbolize an almost deliberate defiance of the encircling gloom. East Berlin is a great deal brighter now than it used to be, but its purely utilitarian illumination is still no match for the exuberant diversity of advertising lights in the West, which takes its cue from Times Square and Piccadilly Circus.

West Berliners love their bright lights as a symbol of their continuing freedom to come and go (more or less) as they please. No matter that the lights are blatant appeals to buy this or that soap, car or deodorant—the West Berliner is happy that, in contrast to the East, so many firms should be competing for his D-marks. Among the most recent additions to this welter of lights is a huge electronic light-board that overlooks the corner of Kurfürstendamm and Joachimsthalerstrasse, the busiest intersection in West Berlin. It is said to have cost several million marks to install—a lot of money for a giant colour television set that plays nothing but commercials. Still, its sponsors seem to be getting their money's worth: visitors from less sophisticated places come to the Kurfürstendamm and stand there gaping at it, "like a cow staring at a new barn door", as the man in the near-by newspaper kiosk once expressed it.

Not only is West Berlin a great deal more fun to live in than the East, it also happens to be the more beautiful part of the city. When Berlin was divided among the victors of the Second World War, the Western Allies received what really amounts to the lion's share, in spite of the fact

An amputated fragment of façade, facing a vacant lot, is all that remains of Berlin's bombed-out Anhalter station, once a gateway to the centre of Germany's capital. Now it stands in the Western half of the city, near the Wall, while over its brick arches loom the steel-and-glass structures of the new West Berlin.

that the Soviets took over the old government and commercial centre. West Berlin, radiating in a great fan shape from the old centre, includes in its outer reaches numerous parks, forests and lakes that give it a pleasantly rural character. On paper it may look like a scattering of garden suburbs. In reality only the outer city is garden-like or suburban. The inner districts close to the Wall are much more heavily populated and contain all you might expect of a long established city centre—department stores, offices, cafés and nightclubs, old squares and crowded tenements—everything, in fact, that West Berlin needs to function as a city within a city, independently of the rest.

In the inner city, the districts nearest to the Wall are the old working-class boroughs of Wedding, Tiergarten and Kreuzberg, forming a semi-circle round the original Berlin city centre but separated from it now by the line of concrete and razed earth. The Wall is not a smooth, rational thing neatly dividing the city. It zigzags and meanders, following municipal boundaries drawn arbitrarily years ago, long before anyone ever dreamed they would become a quasi-international border. In some places the Wall was driven through houses, the DDR portions of which have now been torn down. In other places, such as the Heidelbergerstrasse, the Wall runs down the middle of a street. Occasionally it follows the bank of a river or a canal, and the bridges that used to lead across to streets on the other side now terminate abruptly in concrete barriers—symbols of futility. Gazing down from the air, it is almost as though you were looking at a huge map on which someone had outlined West Berlin's outer limits with a border shown in low relief. This highly artistic "shadow" effect is created by the empty strip behind the Wall, ploughed up in 1961, courtesy of the then DDR Party chief Walter Ulbricht.

The groundplan of the inner city is completed by the elegant commercial and residential boroughs of Schöneberg and Charlottenburg, which lie farther west from the Wall. This part of Berlin had been preferred as a residential district ever since the beginning of the Industrial Revolution, for the prevailing winds are westerlies that blow the smoke and soot from the factory chimneys of Tempelhof and Neukölln over into the eastern areas of the city. In the early 20th Century, Berlin had shifted increasingly westwards; people who could afford it moved to the fringes of the Tiergarten and the Grunewald. Stores, theatres, hotels and restaurants followed them out beyond the Brandenburg Gate, the triumphal arch that marks the edge of the old city centre. The Kurfürstendamm emerged not only as the most fashionable shopping avenue but also as the main street of the New Babylon, where writers and artists, journalists, film directors and dancing girls could all be seen at work or play until the early hours of the morning. "West Berlin" thus had a centre of its own and a spiritual identity even before political events turned it into an island city.

The Kurfürstendamm is now the heartline of inner West Berlin, a

West Berlin's light-beaded avenues radiate outwards from the Kaiser Wilhelm Memorial Church, a war-bombed ruin to which a modern tower was added in the 1960s.

civilized and convivial boulevard not unlike the Champs-Élysées but much longer—3.5 kilometres to be exact, or just over two miles—and less formal. It is the Boulevard St-Michel, Place Pigalle and Champs-Élysées all rolled into one, and one of the few places in Germany where you could, for a moment, imagine yourself in Paris. In the 16th Century it was laid out as a *Dammweg*—a path along an embankment—leading from the inner city to the Elector Joachim II's hunting lodge in the Grunewald: hence the name Kurfürstendamm, the Elector's Embankment. (An elector was one of seven peers entitled to vote whenever a Holy Roman Emperor was to be chosen.) Nowadays Berliners rarely go to the trouble of pronouncing the full name: it's Ku-damm for short.

In summer Berliners go strolling down the Ku-damm or sun themselves in the open-air cafés; in winter they go dodging in and out of its shops and cinemas, bundled up against the cold front that has just rolled in from Siberia. Most of the buildings that stood here in the Twenties and Thirties are long since gone, but not the dynamic atmosphere of the place where the American novelist Thomas Wolfe experienced "the singing of the air by day, the unheard singing of the blood, and the great crowds thronging the Kurfürstendamm, the gay and crowded terraces of the great cafés, and something half-heard, half-suspected, coming from afar, a few seeds of golden notes upon the air, the sudden music of the tootling fifes. . . . "

I have vivid memories of that pre-war Ku-damm, in particular the intersection with the Joachimsthalerstrasse where the giant light-board flashes its electronic messages. This corner was known in the Twenties as the Grünfeld-Ecke, because my great-grandfather's name, F. V. Grünfeld, was boldly emblazoned in art-deco letters across the building that housed the Kurfürstendamm branch of my family's textile firm, which wove linens in Silesia and sold them throughout Germany. The kaisers had bought their shirts and sheets and underpants from F. V. Grünfeld since the mid-19th Century. There was a statue of Wilhelm I in the foyer of the main textile mill in Landeshut, Silesia; and the letters of marque appointing the firm Purveyors of Underwear, or whatever, to His Imperial Majesty were still displayed at the main Berlin store, a massive 19th-Century edifice that stood on the Leipzigerstrasse, just inside what is now East Berlin.

The Kurfürstendamm branch, on the other hand, was an avant-garde establishment very much in keeping with the spirit of the Bauhaus Twenties. Designed by the architect Otto Firle, it had a marvellous spiral staircase wrapped around a tubular lift-shaft of glass and chrome steel—an architectural *tour de force* that allowed you to see through the interior of the building as you rode in the lift from floor to floor. Berlin used to buy its trousseaus there, its bathing suits and table linens, although all I remember of the business is the slogan: "*Weihnachtsgeschenke müssen von Grünfeld sein!*" (Christmas presents have to come from Grünfeld's!)

What made the biggest impression on me as a six- or seven-year-old

In the cobbled plaza of a rebuilt area of West Berlin, the stylized stride of a modern sculpture is unconsciously matched by a passer-by. The sculpture adds to the functional architecture a lightheartedly surrealistic touch that is also apt for a pedestrian precinct.

was the magic fountain in the basement that dispensed lemonade instead of water. There was something about that fountain that captured the imagination of Berliners. I still meet people now and then who confess to having gone there, as children, just to drink the free lemonade—and without having bought anything. The confession usually fills them with remorse all these years later: such are the workings of the guilt complex. They always assume that I must have had *carte blanche* to go there and drink the free lemonade, but that was not at all the case. I did so only twice. My mother had given me strict instructions not to go there by myself, and on the rare occasions when I was taken to Grünfeld's, under escort, it was to order shirts, or pyjamas, or some such, not to drink the lemonade. (Hadn't we lemonade enough at home?) Once, however, I remember my father taking me to drink at the *Limonadenquelle* (the fountain had been his idea, originally, and he took a proprietary interest in it). Once after that, disregarding my mother's instructions, a friend and I managed to sneak past the doorman and down to the lemonade fountain, where we duly guzzled as much lemonade as a body can stand. It seems to me now that I can still taste its delicious, undoubtedly artificial, flavour.

If adventure is what you came for, the Ku-damm is still the place to plunge into the maelstrom of modern Berlin: to meet an employee of the

Colonel's Topographic Survey, a reporter from *Izvestia*, or an argumentative but withal co-operative girl—perhaps, if you are very lucky, all three in one. On the other hand, if you choose the wrong café, you may meet nothing but ladies of a certain age and *embonpoint* with (as Frau Schmidt would say) "time dangling from their fingers"—all consuming their afternoon *Kaffee* and inevitable chocolate *Torte* with whipped cream. If Balzac were alive today and living in Berlin, he would be writing not about *la femme de trente ans* but about *la femme de soixante-sept ans*: that seems to be the median age for the customer at Möhring's chain of cafés. At any one of them you can see table after table occupied by women in the first bloom of old age, living on their well-earned government pensions.

At the end of the war these were the formidable women who cleaned up the rubble of demolished Berlin, the famous *Trümmerfrauen* who swept the ruins of the Reich into their buckets and wheelbarrows and trundled them off in hand-carts, to be dumped on the great mountains of rubble which (now landscaped and planted with grass and trees) have noticeably altered the topography of the city. The poet Goethe once remarked of Berliners that they were "*ein verwegener Menschenschlag*", "a dauntless breed of humanity", and he might have applied the phrase just to the women if he could have seen them at work in the months after the war.

The rubble-women worked virtually without tools, on short rations and unaided. Their menfolk in those months had not yet begun coming back from the war. Many of the men, indeed, were never to return at all, and the war left Berlin with a population that was 70 per cent female. But these Berlin women had a gift for survival in adversity. They survive to this day, a dauntless breed of widows and single women who constitute a world unto themselves, a society of *alte Tanten*, old aunts who can remember having once been Amazons.

The prevalence of these old ladies with their incredible hats (which look like a mixture of Richard Wagner's beret and a steel helmet, and seem to have been carefully saved from the Twenties and Thirties—or are they authentic reproductions?) has given Berlin the well-deserved reputation for being a sort of old people's home. This ought not be a source of embarrassment to the city (although the authorities sometimes sound rather nervous about it); it takes a really great-hearted, patient and understanding city to give old people their due and to win their respect and affection.

Recent statistics show that more than 20 per cent of West Berlin's population is aged 65 or more, whereas less than 15 per cent of the Federal Republic's total population is of similar age. Moreover, the sexual imbalance of the immediate post-war years has not wholly disappeared, and for every 1,000 men in the city there are still almost 1,300 women. These figures are largely explained by West Berlin's uncertain post-war status. Young Berliners who felt they had nothing to expect of the future

A rooftop car park (right) and a startling red capsule that houses a variety of restaurants (above) are among the elevated amenities offered to West Berliners who shop or work in this ambitious complex of 150 shops and businesses opened in 1970. Located in the suburb of Steglitz, it underlines Berlin's tendency—dating from long before the city's division—to develop outwards and westwards, away from the grime of its old industrial centre.

were understandably quick to leave the city: it was their parents—or, for many, their widowed mothers—who tended to stay on in the place where they had lived all their lives and where they could hear the sweet, familiar intonations of *Berlinerisch*.

The West German "economic miracle" came to West Berlin more slowly than to the rest of the country, but since the war close to 800 million marks in subsidies have been poured into the city every year by the Federal government and, with the gradual disappearance of the older generation, the population pyramid has taken on a more normal shape. "Berlin is again a very prosperous city," I was told by one of the civil servants who work for the Senate. "It's a good place for careers and making money. Young Berliners no longer have to go to the West to improve their prospects; they know they've got a good future if they stay put."

If you are trying to pinpoint the centre of this revitalized city of West Berlin, you could consider the claims of the Breitscheidplatz, which stands where the Kurfürstendamm begins and contains the best-known architectural symbol of West Berlin: the Kaiser Wilhelm Memorial Church. Everybody knows who Kaiser Wilhelm I was: a gentleman with mutton-chop whiskers who was proclaimed Kaiser at Versailles in 1871—grandfather of that "second Wilhelm" who abdicated in 1918. Almost nobody, though, could identify the man after whom the square is named. Rudolf Breitscheid was one of the leaders of the Social Democratic Party and a minister during the Weimar Republic, who lost his life in a Nazi concentration camp during the Second World War. The square thus manages to commemorate two quite separate and distinct directions in the history of recent German politics.

Kaiser Wilhelm's Memorial, before the war, was an enormous church in the neo-Romanesque style of the 1890s, whose huge cupola loomed over the beginnings of the Ku-damm like the Ghost of Christmas Past. The Second World War left it in ruins, and the post-war controversy over whether the blackened remains should be torn down or built up was resolved with a typical Berlin compromise. The hideous ruins—particularly so because the original building was a monstrosity—were left standing as a *Mahnmal*, a "warning to posterity" (moral: don't get bombed), and a modern architect, Professor Egon Eiermann, attached a modern, glass-and-concrete church to the side of the old that strikes me as no great improvement over what was there before. The fact that the waffle-like exterior resembles an egg crate, and that the architect's name means "egg-man", has not been lost on the impious Berliners, who invariably have a smart-aleck nickname for everything: they call it Eiermann's Egg Crate. (The old part of the church is known as The Hollow Tooth.) But inside the church, the sun shining through the purple-blue stained glass windows casts a profoundly melancholy light on the octagonal space dedicated to

As clerks update share quotations projected on the wall, three bankers and two brokers take part in the lively trading at West Berlin's new Stock Exchange.

the memory of the Christian martyrs who died resisting the Nazis. As for the Hohenzollern dynasty, whose royal chapel once stood here, they are still remembered in a very subtle fashion: the carillon in the new bell-tower plays a melody composed by Prince Louis Ferdinand of Prussia, the present head of the Hohenzollern family and a namesake of the Prussian prince who distinguished himself as a composer in Beethoven's day.

On the whole it is not a terribly prepossessing place, this Breitscheidplatz: its only other distinguishing feature is the sprawling Europa Center, surmounted by a giant revolving replica of the three-pointed Mercedes-Benz radiator-cap insignia. Someone designed this building to be the commercial rabbit-warren of all time. It houses dozens of cafés, restaurants, cabarets and shops (there is said to be more than a mile of display windows): it has an all-year indoor ice-rink, a swimming pool, thermal baths like those of the spa at Baden-Baden, a Finnish sauna, a medical polyclinic, art galleries and a rooftop restaurant with 30,000 square feet of terrace garden—all this in the place where the poets and painters of Berlin used to foregather at the famous Romanisches Café, which was closed at the start of the war and then bombed out. There is still a café by that name in the Europa Center, but it has about as much in common with the original Romanisches as a currywurst has with a Bismarck herring. The rest of the square is taken up by shops and office buildings, travel agencies, beer cellars and the Berlin branch of a prominent chain of sex shops, virtually a Sexual Liberation Front.

This square, for all practical purposes, can be regarded as the centre of West Berlin. Actually, the city fathers have yet to recognize it as such. Other European cities all have signposts pointing the way to their town centre; in West Berlin there are no such aids to the wayfarer. If you're looking for the centre, follow the signs reading "*Zoo*". The signs that say "*Mitte*", i.e. the middle of town, refer to the old centre of Berlin and will lead you to East Berlin. One has to understand this strange code, which reflects the fact that the West has not yet conceded that Berlin is divided, and that the erstwhile *Mitte* is no longer the functioning *Mitte* of the whole city.

This, surely, is the only major city in the world whose designated centre is the Zoo. The Zoologische Garten, as it happens, once lay beyond the precincts of central Berlin; but fate, or history, has brought its monkeys and lions a prominence and immediacy they never thought to attain. Since the zoo lies just a few steps from the business district around the Breitscheidplatz, many Berliners think nothing of taking their lunch hour there, to make faces at the orang-utan or watch the seals being fed. On moonlit nights, as you wander along the boulevards near the zoo, you can sometimes hear the wolves baying at the moon, and the coyotes howling.

Berliners are inordinately proud of their zoo. I say inordinately because the whole business of keeping animals in captivity has always seemed cruel to me; and, in Berlin, the sight of these caged creatures reminds you

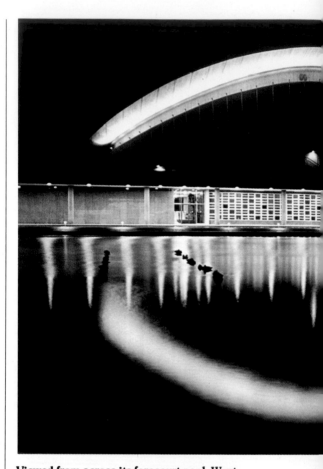

Viewed from across its forecourt pool, West Berlin's Congress Hall in the Tiergarten gapes—as local wags observe—like a "pregnant oyster". The hall, which includes theatres, exhibition spaces, a restaurant and an outdoor café, was built in 1957 as the American contribution to the International Building Exhibition—a significant event in the city's reconstruction after the war.

all too forcibly that this is the city of walls and fences. Still, Berliners are not inclined to view their zoo metaphorically, and they take their children to see it on regular weekend airings, and to climb on the jungle gyms that a thoughtful municipality has installed there so that young humans can swing from bar to bar, emulating their simian cousins on the other side of the fence. Philosophically, the whole Berlin question keeps coming down to the old conundrum of the zoological garden: who's in and who's out? Who's watching whom? If Robert Frost had come from Berlin, would he still have insisted that "good fences make good neighbours"?

Bahnhof Zoo, the railway station just opposite the main entrance to the zoo, is where you alight if you arrive in West Berlin by train. It may strike you, even on a good day, as the dingiest railway facility this side of the third-class waiting room at Benares—certainly not at all what one would expect from a tourist-minded city that welcomes its visitors so sumptuously at its ultra-modern Tegel airport. But you need not search far for the explanation. By another of the "internal contradictions" for which Berlin has become famous, Bahnhof Zoo belongs to the Reichsbahn, the old German railway system that was taken over by the East Germans after the Second World War.

It is the DDR which administers this island within an island, and since they are not remotely interested in providing amenities for West Berliners, they furnish only minimal upkeep for Reichsbahn facilities in the West. The result is a sort of skid-row enclave, with DDR railway officials in rumpled blue uniforms and a supporting cast of legless veterans, alcoholics and other unfortunates who have made the Bahnhof their permanent home. I think the Reichsbahn people rather enjoy having them there as living examples, straight out of a George Grosz caricature, of what can happen to you in the insecurities of capitalism: you won't find any tramps in DDR railway stations in the East.

The Reichsbahn runs an oddly limited railway system. One day I tried to forward some baggage from Berlin to Barcelona by freight, and discovered that the Reichsbahn could accept shipments only as far as France; it didn't have an agreement with the Spanish railways. This is a terrible come-down for a city that used to boast of having the busiest and best connected railway system in Europe. When I was a boy, Berlin was a speedster's paradise that seemed to have left most of Europe behind in the horse-and-buggy age. I remember going to the Anhalter station, which is near the heart of old Berlin, to watch the great steam and diesel loco-motives start out on their transcontinental runs. It was then the principal railway station in Berlin; now there is nothing left of it but a single wall and the main portico of the entrance, with a few sculptured ladies still perched above the doors. Behind them lie, not tracks or platforms, but a huge vacant lot that is sometimes used as a parking place for buses. More than 250 trains a day used to depart from the five Berlin terminals (not counting suburban lines), destined for places all over Europe; now, both halves of the city can scarcely muster 70 trains a day.

I remember, too, the excitement of actually getting on the trains that would take my sisters and me, and our wonderfully competent governess, on holiday to France or Switzerland—the incredible locomotives, pouring out their anticipatory clouds of steam; the gleaming watch being pulled from the conductor's pocket as a sign that the journey was about to begin; the equally gleaming brass of the fittings in Pullman carriages; the smell of delicious sauces in the mahogany-panelled dining cars, and the endless ostinato rhythm of the wheels on the tracks as I dozed off in my upper berth, knowing that the next day there would be the mountains outside and another landscape, another kind of life. I loved trains to the exclusion of every other form of transport, and I still do. For me the aeroplane will never replace the railway, if only because of the sheer loveliness of rail travel. Am I so wrong?

At any rate, when I was young, I thought of speed as an essential and unique characteristic of Berlin. It seemed to my partial and unpractised eye that Zurich, Paris, even London, moved at a much slower tempo. Not until I got to New York for the first time did I realize that there were cities with an even faster beat than Berlin's. In the city of four million that was the Berlin of my boyhood, everything and everyone seemed to be perpetually on the move: the square green taxis, the *elektrische* trams and double-decker buses on which, as soon as I was allowed out of the house on my own, I used to ride from one end of town to the other; the yellow-and-blue coaches of the spotlessly clean underground U-Bahn with its vast network of 92 stations, and the swift trains of the elevated S-Bahn, which could carry you to romantic-sounding places like Potsdam, Falkensee and Königs Wusterhausen. (The S-Bahn still operates—a much curtailed service, administered parsimoniously by the DDR-owned Reichsbahn.)

At some of the great junctions in the city you could see all the lines coming together, as in a spider's web. Standing on the street, you heard and felt the rumble of the U-Bahn beneath your feet, saw the cars and trucks rolling by, the people jamming trolleys and buses, while overhead there were elevated tracks and railway conduits; as many as three or four trains moving at different levels and in various directions. In the background there was the Radio Funkturm with flashing lights on its transmitter, and aeroplanes from Tempelhof Airfield. It was better than a scene from the advertising films we used to see, gratis, at Sunday-morning matinée performances in the cinemas near the zoo. (Those were true matinées: they were held in the mornings, not like your theatre matinées, which are given in the afternoons.) Berlin now has a million fewer people overall but its tempo, at least in the West, is still the fastest in Central Europe. As soon as you step out of the decrepit zoo station you can feel a quickening of the pulse, the impatient rhythm of traffic along the avenues.

Praised as a model design and damned as a modern slum, West Berlin's Märkisches Viertel development was built in the late 1960s and houses 60,000 people.

One can say of virtually every city that it is a study in contrasts. In West Berlin the contrasts tend to take bizarre and curious forms. About seven minutes' walk from the busiest, noisiest intersections at the "zoo-centre" are some of the quietest, most desolate streets in the whole city. Here, for block after block along the Tiergartenstrasse, are the empty lots and low mounds of rubble overgrown with bushes that are all that is left of the once-proud diplomatic quarter. The area has been reserved for future development should the foreign embassies ever move back to a reunited Berlin. Unlike other devastated areas that were either reconstructed or used for new buildings, the bombed-out ruins of the Tiergartenstrasse were simply razed and allowed to lie fallow. The house at Number 44 where I lived before the war is now a rubble-strewn plot—a few years ago the number was still painted on the pavement in front, but now the plot is unmarked, although it is used for storage by a dealer in building materials.

By an ironic coincidence, what you do still find standing on the Tiergartenstrasse are the once-proud embassies of Nazi Germany's Axis partners, Italy and Japan. These pompous palaces were built in the prevailing Nazi style, complete with colonnades and balconies from which visiting dignitaries could greet the Berlin crowds, Führer-fashion. The war put an end to such pretensions, but in due course these two embassy buildings reverted to their respective successor governments. Since West Berlin is no longer a capital, however, no attempt has been made to restore the embassies as such. Instead, the Italians have tucked their consulate into one small corner of the original structure, with access from a side entrance. The Japanese have renovated only enough rooms to house a caretaker. For the rest, the buildings are gradually going to seed. Windows and portals have been walled up; bushes grow out of the terraces; in winter, icicles drip through the cracked floors of the balconies. Pigeons fly in and out of the shattered windows on the top floors; they roost in what appear to have been rococo-panelled rooms, now in total decay. The symbol of a rising sun still adorns the Japanese embassy, but no flag flutters from the flagpole on top of the building; instead I have seen rabbits in the garden behind the house, where the caretaker also has a chicken coop.

The former Spanish embassy at the end of the Tiergartenstrasse has also fallen on hard times. Several rooms are currently in use as the consulate, but the rest of the building is as derelict as the others. Part of it was destroyed during the war; a corner has been cut out of it and the walls have been shored up. But the great Falangist coat of arms still dominates the front of the building; and the windows, although bricked up, are barred with elaborate wrought-iron grilles, some of them bearing the Falangist symbol, the yoke and the arrows, although time and shell splinters have knocked out some of the arrows. I can imagine the embarrassment of having to operate from a mousehole in this monumental piece of fantasy architecture, with symbols of past glories plastered all over it, mute

In Kreuzberg, a district of West Berlin near the Wall, the son of a Turkish immigrant worker apes the soldiers he sees so often. Turks, living chiefly in Kreuzberg, form the largest group among the Gastarbeiter (guest workers) who were brought in during the late 1960s to meet the city's chronic labour shortage.

testimony to having backed the wrong side. Moreover, these diplomatic palaces of the Reich now stand revealed as having been built of brick with façades of stucco, patches of which have come off, with an indescribably shabby effect. They have the air of World's Fair pavilions that have been left over after the fair has closed.

Indeed, these buildings and a few better preserved relics—notably the huge 1936 Olympic Stadium on the road to Spandau—are all that remain of Adolf Hitler's scheme for a glorified Berlin that was to serve as a lasting memorial "to the might achieved by the Hitler era". Fortunately, most of Hitler's plans for a monster new capital never got off the drawing-boards. As his ex-architect, Albert Speer, has described them in his memoirs, Hitler's plans called for the centre of the city to be dominated by a series of huge buildings, of which the largest was to be a domed, 180,000-seat Assembly Hall—"the greatest assembly hall in the world"—with a cupola four times the size of the U.S. Capitol. Designed to be the centre of the Nazi quasi-religious cult, it would, according to Speer, "over the course of the centuries . . . acquire an importance similar to that which St. Peter's in Rome has for Catholic Christianity". The vast dome was to be surmounted by a gargantuan German eagle perched on a globe of the world. "Here we no longer want the eagle standing over the swastika," Hitler told Speer. "Here he will master the globe. The crowning of this biggest building in the world must be the eagle over the globe."

Hitler and his architects wanted everything in Berlin to be huge, clean, geometric and predictable. The very antithesis of that sort of town planning—and its most convincing antidote—can be found in Kreuzberg, the old workers' district which lies only half a dozen U-Bahn stops from the centre of town. Kreuzberg has long been the most densely populated borough of West Berlin. Here the streets are narrow, the houses low and sagging with age. Yet this is the warmest and most vivid part of the city, the area most favoured by landscape painters. Much of it, although dirty and decrepit, is exceptionally beautiful.

Many parts of this borough give the impression that you have suddenly been wafted to the Near East; tens of thousands of its inhabitants are Turkish *Gastarbeiter* ("guest workers") who have brought their wives and families with them from the old country. Some sections of Kreuzberg, where the stores are called *souks* and all the signs are in Turkish, have taken on an Arabian Nights atmosphere, and the music that wafts from the open windows is far more oriental than anything Richard Strauss composed for the *Dance of the Seven Veils.*

Some areas of Kreuzberg may remind you, too, of the older districts of Paris. The Chamissoplatz, for example (named after the French-born poet, Adelbert von Chamisso, who is buried in Kreuzberg Cemetery along with the composer Felix Mendelssohn and the Romantic author E. T. A. Hoffmann), is a square that might have been bodily transported from the Marais, in Paris. It is surrounded by tenement houses on all sides, but flanked by birch and willow trees, with a playground in the middle, an old horse-pump and water-trough on one side and a cast-iron *pissoir* on the other. I saw a sign tacked to one of the birches: "*Bad zwecks Umzug günstig zu verkaufen.*" (Moving: bath for sale, cheap.) Among the small shops near by is an old cellar depot that sells coal and coke to people who still have stoves instead of central heating. The coal comes in long briquets, and these fit into special crates holding about a hundredweight, which are carried up five or six flights of stairs by delivery men with the muscles of Sherpa mountain guides.

Over the years there has been a lot of well-intentioned hand-wringing over the plight of the migrant workers in their crowded tenements, and the need to construct modern housing for them. But when a survey was conducted to find out what the Kreuzbergers wanted for themselves, it was discovered that the Turks were happy here, where they could live in quasi-Mediterranean surroundings, in protective, old-fashioned houses with cave-like rooms. They liked proximity and human contact, and were

Beside the wine barrels in the courtyard of a West Berlin Kneipe, three delivery men shoulder racks full of pressed brown coal briquets. Widely used in open fires and coal ovens in both halves of Berlin, the briquets are very brittle and soon disintegrate if they are not carried in the racks and handled with great care.

understandably reluctant to exchange their comfortable community for the antiseptic blocks of new flats under construction on the outskirts of town. What they really wanted were better social services and a chance to improve the old houses, not tear them down. Whether good sense will prevail in this matter remains to be seen; Kreuzberg may yet be saved from the modern architects.

Whatever happens, the city fathers in their planning for the future will have to respect the new force represented by the Turkish *Gastarbeiter*. By the mid-1970s almost 100,000 immigrant Turks had come to Berlin, along with lesser thousands of Yugoslavs, Greeks, Italians and Spaniards. They came because Berlin industries were badly short-handed and paid them substantial bonuses. But what began as a temporary expedient has become a long-range influence on the city's *persona*. The Turks and the other migrant workers have been giving West Berlin a badly needed infusion of young blood. (Statisticians reveal that in recent years one of every five babies born in West Berlin had Turkish parents.) And the Turkish presence, which has created many tensions over the years, has also had a noticeable and positive effect on life in West Berlin.

For one thing, the change in local eating habits is nothing short of phenomenal. Turkish restaurants are everywhere, providing an exotic and inexpensive alternative to the conventional cooking of the land, which until recently consisted mainly of six kinds of sausages. Now shish kebab has become so much a staple of the Berlin diet that even the ordinary Imbiss stands on the street corners—small huts on wheels designed for the stand-as-you-eat consumption of sausages, cakes, drinks and other miscellaneous delicacies—carry skewers of kebab, ready to be grilled to your order. Not even the Huguenots, who brought the city its special *Berliner Weisse*, or white beer, have made a more profound contribution to the community's gastronomical melting pot.

In Kreuzberg the Turkish influence touches even the most Germanic of the district's monuments, the Kreuzberg itself—the Mount of the Cross after which the borough is named—which marks the highest natural elevation in the inner city. Once a vineyard, the hill is now a park, and on its summit, 217 feet above sea-level, stands a neo-Gothic monument to that most Prussian of endeavours, the war against Napoleon. The names and dates of the major battles are inscribed on the monument—Leipzig, Dennewitz, Gross Beeren, Katzbach—along with a message from the King of Prussia thanking his subjects for sacrificing *Gut und Blut* (life and property) for the Fatherland, and enjoining future generations to follow their stirring example. Now the present generation of Kreuzbergers have added their own names and heroes, in the form of graffiti, to the proud old battle honours of the Prussian host: "Ahmet Demir, Gazikly, Aynur & Mehmet, Ataturk, Ankara, Adana, Hakkeym. . . . "

Kreuzberg has much in common with Neukölln, a neighbouring district which, although not so densely populated, ranks as the most populous borough in the city. It has nearly 300,000 residents, many of them also *Gastarbeiter*. Both districts lie next to the Wall and both contain fertile ground for a proper Berlin *Bummel*, a *Bummel* being a casual stroll through town that has no definite destination; the only condition being that you amuse yourself along the way.

A good place to *bummel* on the western margins of Neukölln is the Tempelhof area. In the Middle Ages the land was held by the Knights Templar and in the days of the kaisers it was used as an exercise field for the Grenadiers of the Berlin garrison. Converted from parade ground to airfield after the First World War, it gained new importance during the Soviet blockade of West Berlin in 1948-49, when it received most of the two million tons of food and supplies flown in by the Western Allies.

At the entrance to Tempelhof Airfield, which is now used mainly for U.S. military flights, there is a three-pronged "Airlift Memorial", symbolizing the three Western air corridors to Berlin, and popularly referred to as *Die Hungerharke* ("Hunger's Pitchfork"). The siege it commemorates now seems very long ago. The Berlin children playing soccer in the open field across the street from Tempelhof have never known anything of hunger or unheated winters. Indeed, the scene rather reminds me of Harrow, with its lush, green playing fields, the steeple of a church in the background and the sound of bells in the air.

Much more representative of modern Berlin is the *Gropiusstadt*, or Gropius City, where about 50,000 of Neukölln's inhabitants live in towering apartment blocks that look, from a distance, like a modern Camelot. Officially known as the Berlin-Buckow-Rudow Housing Development, it was designed and supervised by the grand old man of Bauhaus architecture, Walter Gropius, who returned periodically in the 1960s from his American exile (where he was professor at the Harvard School of Architecture) to help rebuild the city of his birth.

Personally, I prefer to *bummel* in the older parts of Neukölln, along the quays and canals, and through the back streets near the Wall (known variously as the "sector boundary" or the "state frontier" depending on which side you happen to be standing). One of these back streets, the Heidelbergerstrasse, is literally split in half by the Wall; but unlike other Berlin streets thus afflicted, the houses on the Eastern side have been neither torn down nor bricked up. Here the whole absurdity of the Berlin situation takes the form of a neighbourhood tragedy.

The Wall runs down the middle of what used to be quite a broad street, leaving sufficient room for a few trees as well as a pavement on the Western side. Through cracks in the Wall you can see an empty, ploughed strip and some wire fencing on the far side; then houses, exactly like the ones on the Western side, vintage 1900. Laundry is drying on several balconies. An old lady leans out of the third-floor window; she can look over the Wall and watch the comings and goings on the Western pavement. An old couple (West) walk down the street arm in arm; they wave to her (East); and she waves back. Do they know each other, or is it only a reflex action? They may even be related: some 800,000 West Berliners have close relatives on the other side of the Wall.

The Heidelbergerstrasse is otherwise unremarkable: a couple of pubs, a *Parfümerie*, a shop for *Tabakwaren & Spirituosen*, the curtained ground-floor windows of somebody's living room through which you can see a teddy bear, potted plants, a cluster of plastic mushrooms, red with white polka dots. There is little here to suggest that we are standing at the Great Divide, the new frontier between the Eastern and the Western worlds.

In the busier of the two neighbourhood pubs the old American Western series, *Bonanza*, is showing on the TV. A tipsy customer who identifies himself as a philosopher grabs me round the neck as I enter and reminds me about the necessity of loving one's neighbour. The barman, a young man with a drooping moustache, pulls him back: "Albert, stop butting in where you're not wanted." Albert and several others gradually subside into a beery stupor. A restless young Turk is seated at the bar, and two hardware salesmen in green shirts are talking earnestly with a woman in a print dress. There are several oil paintings on the wall: three landscapes, a flower painting, two horse pictures and a portrait of Otto von Bismarck. A wagon wheel has been wired up as a ceiling light fixture; there is a tiled coke stove in the corner, a pinball machine, and a slot machine.

The TV is turned off. A minor character in the show has died, and that ends the episode. Albert turns to the jukebox and plays the same song again and again until the barman tells him to stop. When the young Turk gets up to leave, the door flies open and there, not five feet away, is the relentless concrete of the Wall; in the window of the house just behind it, somebody's laundry is flapping in the breeze. When I myself get up to leave, the philosopher has returned to the subject of brotherly love, but nobody's listening. Not far away, where the Wall runs close to a small Catholic church, somebody has placed two lighted candles in a niche beside the Wall to commemorate some escapee shot by the DDR border guards. Children are skipping and playing beside it. It's a safe street for kids: no through traffic.

3

Country in the City

Newcomers are always surprised to find that, instead of being the cramped, embattled outpost they expected to encounter, West Berlin is about as comfortable as an old shoe. Beyond the crowded neighbourhoods at the centre of the city, West Berlin is really a community of suburbs, or—better said—a collection of towns and villages, each very different from the next, held together by the strands of its superbly functioning network of trains and buses. It is an astonishingly green place, this outer city, generously endowed with parks, lakes and forests that go on and on, seemingly without end. "You mean we're still in West Berlin?" visiting friends usually ask in astonishment when I take them for a drive in the western outskirts. Here in the green belt and the "lake district" it seems impossible that we could still be within the city limits.

On one route you cross the River Havel on a small car ferry, then meander through pine woods and past farms to a village—Heiligensee—whose gabled houses would not look out of place in New England. Deer live in these forests, and even a few wild boar. The lakes are stocked with fish (West Berlin has more than 20,000 licensed anglers). There are hiking trails on which you can spend the whole day without seeing a car. The Berlin Pflanzenschutzamt (Plant Protection Bureau) puts out a pamphlet identifying the 27 varieties of edible mushrooms that can be collected in the city's woods. And in outlying villages like Lübars and Heiligensee, a dwindling but persistent minority of farmers maintain small dairy herds or grow rye for "country-style" loaves.

But sooner or later you come up against the inevitable. It is a curious sensation: you're driving along a highway, through fields or scattered settlements, and suddenly you run up against the "country" Wall (the distinction is made by the British Army in Berlin, which assigns separate patrols to the "city" and the "country" Walls in its sector). The atmosphere out here is not quite as sinister as in the centre, but the underlying reality is the same: once more you find yourself within machine-gun range of a watch-tower. *Achtung!* Warning! Do not proceed beyond this point! As you turn and drive along one of the roads running parallel to the fence you will be watched all the way by DDR guards using binoculars. And your visitor at last will be in no doubt that he has reached the city limits of West Berlin.

The innermost part of the green belt is the Grunewald district, which begins where the Kurfürstendamm comes to an end. You enter the Grunewald through the Rathenauplatz. Walther Rathenau was a millionaire writer and philosopher who became Foreign Minister of the Weimar Republic in 1922

Pleasure craft clutter the forested shores of the River Havel and its inlets, which lace the boundaries of outer West Berlin. These and other waterways combine with woods and farms to create the sweeping rural landscapes that make up 35 per cent of West Berlin's land area.

only to be killed later that year, not far from this square named in his honour (at the corner of the Königsallee and Wallotstrasse). His murderers were proto-Nazis, although their politics were not yet known by that name, and it was here they served notice on the world that reactionary nationalism was a living force in Germany and a threat to peace in Europe. The square itself is not nearly as momentous as the event it commemorates; in fact, it could easily be mistaken for a mere traffic circle. Not that it matters. After all, Berlin is full of places where people were assassinated, tortured, maimed: if there were to be suitable memorials to all of them, there would not be room for much else.

The Grunewald district lies immediately behind the Rathenauplatz. It is one of the most remarkable residential suburbs in the world, an area of trees and gardens, with sumptuous turn-of-the-century villas set on the shores of small lakes conveniently left behind by the last Ice Age. All this is within 10 minutes' drive of the city centre.

I have fond memories of one of these lakes, the Hundekehlesee (Lake of the Dog's Gullet), because that is where I learned to swim. My uncle George and Aunt Edith had a villa there overlooking the lake, and my grandmother also lived there, as a widow, in the gardener's cottage on their estate. We would visit them at weekends or on a sunny afternoon, and my good-natured aunt agreed to teach me to swim. As I recall (perhaps it was not precisely like this) I had been taught the motions on dry land with no more than a stroke or two in the bathtub to get an idea of the real thing. The lake bottom was too muddy to permit wading in from the shore. Instead, we went out in a rowing boat; my Aunt Edith tied a rope around my waist and then invited me to jump in (or was I pushed?). She pulled on the oars and the boat moved out of my reach. The rope jerked and started to drag me under. I tried to shout for help, found myself gargling in the water of the Hundekehlessee, struggled, saw my short life (I was only six) pass before my eyes. Suddenly my amphibian instincts took hold. I kicked out my hind legs, raised my chin long enough to take a breath, moved my arms as I had been told, and swam triumphantly after the boat. Aunt Edith finally had to haul me back in, her educational methods vindicated.

Now when I look at the Hundekehlesee, I still get a sinking sensation in the pit of my stomach, and the image of that house on the shore—with its spacious terraces, its pergolas and gazebos—rises in my mind's eye like Scarlett O'Hara's plantation in *Gone with the Wind*. I saw it again after the war. My aunt's secretary was living in the gardener's cottage, but I could not set foot in the house itself; it had been rented by the government of West Germany to serve as the official residence of the *Bundespräsident*—at that time Theodor Heuss—during his visits to West Berlin. Subsequently the official Berlin residence of the President of the Federal Republic was moved to the newly restored Bellevue Palace in the Tiergarten, where instead of the lake associated with my early triumphs he could look out upon the

On the outskirts of West Berlin there are more than a hundred farms supplying food to the city, and the rural life-style is surprisingly prevalent even in the central districts. This cow is being led into a dairy in Schöneberg that keeps a herd in its back yard. Inside the dairy (left) a worker washes out cans and pails.

English Garden presented to the city by the Shropshire Horticultural Society; it was opened by Britain's wartime Foreign Secretary, Anthony Eden, with gifts of plants from the gardens of the British royal family.

Once the Bellevue Palace was ready, my late uncle's villa, beautiful as a dream of paradise, was torn down to make way for something concrete and rectilinear. All that is left as a memento is a gazebo near the lakeshore, and a few of the old weeping willows at the spot where my sisters and cousins used to sit on the landing stage kicking up spray with their toes. I don't go swimming there any more, but sometimes, on a winter visit, I'll join the skaters to take a few turns round the ice.

If you drive for five miles through the Grunewald Forest—more than 15 square miles of pines and birch trees, interrupted only by a few roads, a lake or two, an old royal hunting lodge and such—you will come to the banks of the River Havel, where it widens into a lake of spacious proportions. On a hill overlooking the river, Friedrich Wilhelm III in 1819 built the Russian-style log house of Nikolskoe for his daughter Charlotte, wife of the Grand Duke Nicholas, later Czar. Today this pleasure palace has been converted into a restaurant from whose terraces you can enjoy a sweeping view not only of the river but also of the DDR countryside beyond the Wall. The neighbouring church of St. Peter and St. Paul, with its onion-shaped tower, completes the illusion that you have somehow stumbled on to a piece of 19th-Century Russian landscape straight out of Dostoevsky—only the sonic background of the interminable talk among the Berliners seems out of key with the rest.

Amid the greenery of the Pfaueninsel on the River Havel are fake ruins of a "Medieval" castle and other royal follies built in the 18th and 19th Centuries.

Near by, in the river itself, you can visit the enchanted Pfaueninsel (Peacock Island) which lies not much more than a stone's throw from the bank and is reached by means of a small passenger ferry. At the landing stage a welcoming committee of peacocks awaits you, summer and winter. The peacocks have the run of the island, and so do you, provided you pick no flowers nor pluck any peacock feathers. I remember going there with my father, more than 40 years ago, and finding one small iridescent feather in the underbrush. On the return trip, instead of keeping it in my pocket, I proudly showed it to the men who ran the boat; they confiscated it in the name of the law. It was, of course, *verboten* to remove so much as a pin-feather from the precincts of the Pfaueninsel, and still is.

You are well advised to visit this spot, however, not just for the peacocks but for the dream-like landscape afforded by the island itself—a romantic blend of oak forest, open meadow and fantasy castles, like a setting for *A Midsummer Night's Dream*. Strolling through the woods, you catch glimpses of a far-off towering *Lustschloss*, or pleasure palace, built in the 1790s for the Countess Lichtenau, the mistress of King Friedrich Wilhelm II. Elsewhere in this royal amusement park there is a "Swiss Cottage" and a "Guest House", a "Dairy" resembling a half-ruined castle, a Greek temple commemorating the much-beloved Queen Luise of Prussia, and other intriguing relics of a time when architecture was a game to be played by royal dilettantes and their favourite court designers. You can while away a Sunday afternoon on this enchanted island (it is about a mile and a half long) and scarcely notice the ugly concrete wall that runs along the other bank of the Havel, barring the old royal route to the palace at Potsdam. But the wall is there, a jarring note of harsh reality—and a reminder that Peacock Island and the neighbouring shores have been the settings for ugly incidents at times in the past.

The guidebooks say a great deal about the royal history of the Pfaueninsel, but they neglect to mention the bizarre episode that occurred here during the Nazi epoch. In the summer of 1936, when the Olympic Games were held in Berlin, Hitler's Minister for Popular Enlightenment and Propaganda, Dr. Goebbels, decided to throw a gala garden party on the Pfaueninsel. For the occasion, a pontoon bridge was built by Wehrmacht engineers so that the 3,000 guests could walk on to the island instead of waiting for the ferry. The guest list included leading figures in the German government, the entire diplomatic corps, generals of the army and admirals of the fleet, café society, stars of stage and screen, members of the old noblesse, industrialists, and Olympic athletes; and also some of the old Stormtroop captains— veterans of beer-hall brawls and street fighting, who were now ensconced as government functionaries.

Dr. Goebbels, the overlord not only of the Press but also of the Reich's theatres, was determined to dramatize the elegance and splendour of which the Nazi regime was capable. The island's footpaths were illuminated by

On a hot July weekend thousands of West Berliners crowd what is said to be the largest inland bathing beach in Europe: the Strandbad, on the Grosser Wannsee. Brisk, prevailing westerly winds make the lake a sailing centre, but to avoid the breezes many bathers loll in protective basket chairs hired by the day.

torches held aloft by rows of nubile dancing girls dressed as rococo page boys in powdered wigs, silk blouses and tight-fitting trousers. The trees were festooned with thousands of lights; the tables in the refreshment pavilions were heaped high with lobster, pheasant and caviar; dance bands played music for three outdoor dance arenas, and waiters in tails passed among the guests pouring out an endless stream of champagne.

Then the torch-bearing pages began mingling with the guests. It soon became apparent that, while some pages might have been drawn from the corps de ballet of the Staatsoper, most had been recruited in cabarets and music halls. According to the biographers of Magda Goebbels, the minister's wife, the tone of the occasion quickly deteriorated: "Before long, one saw drunken, reeling figures with shrieking girls under their arms or on their knees, trying to make off with them into the underbrush. Adjutants feverishly tried to maintain order, and fretful aides from the ministry did their best to pacify the spirits that had been aroused. But the strong-arm men from the beer-hall brawls of north-east Berlin had learned long ago how to defend themselves against outside interference. Jaws were punched, people were kicked; bottles flew through the air. A few hearty spirits began pushing over the tables, whereupon the ambassadors, ministers, generals and captains of industry took flight. Thus Goebbels' feast on the Pfaueninsel turned into the greatest scandal of Berlin during the Third Reich. Magda wept for shame. The minister was in a rage, the Führer indignant."

Six years later a much more decorous and successful party was held on the shores of the Grosser Wannsee, an inlet of the River Havel two miles

away from the Pfaueninsel. On January 20, 1942, SS *Obergruppenführer* Reinhard Heydrich convened a conference of government and SS officials in a villa at 56-58 Am Grossen Wannsee. Over a convivial lunch these 15 men evolved the "Final Solution of the Jewish question". Adolf Eichmann, head of the "Jewish Section" of the Gestapo, took the minutes. Having completed their agenda, Heydrich and his guests sat around the fireplace, smoking, drinking cognac and, according to Eichmann, "not just talking shop but giving ourselves a rest after so many taxing hours".

If you were to sail a boat northwards up the River Havel to the point where it joins the Spree, you would arrive in Spandau, the westernmost borough of West Berlin. Spandau is where the Nazi war leaders sentenced at Nuremberg were held prisoner in a pseudo-medieval, red-brick fortress guarded by each of the four occupying powers for a month at a time. When I was last there it was still being run as a maximum security jail, not so much to keep in its solitary surviving prisoner, Rudolf Hess, as to keep out journalists, tourists and curiosity-seekers; even taking a picture of the gate was *verboten* by the authorities.

Most visitors to Spandau, as it happens, confuse the Nazi war criminals' 19th-Century penitentiary with the 16th-Century Citadel of Spandau: a castle with a massive crenellated tower, exactly like a rook in a chess set, which lies on the opposite bank of the river. The citadel is not a prison nowadays, but during its long history many celebrated prisoners were incarcerated here—including the beautiful Anna Sydow, mistress of the 16th-Century Elector Joachim II, whose son locked her up for life in the tower as soon as his father had died.

Joachim II was both a great lover and a merry soul, known to be fond of practical jokes. In August, 1567, he had the good burghers of Spandau hauled out of their beds, armed with wooden spears and shields, and sent out on the river in small boats to meet a contingent of Berliners, similarly equipped, in a mock naval battle. The two towns were then bitter rivals and what ensued was a great cracking of skulls. But the issue remained un-decided until the Elector ordered the battle to be continued on dry land, and here the Spandauers routed the Berliners. Meanwhile, Joachim had decided to escalate the fun by ordering his artillerymen to train the citadel's cannon on Spandau, whereupon they opened fire on the old St. Nicholas Church. The brick walls of the church were severely damaged before the Spandau town council could prevail on Joachim to stop. Apparently he resented the fact that the church steeple was higher than the tower of his own citadel.

If you visit the citadel, you may wonder why the walls of the former officers' club contain so many stones with Hebrew inscriptions. They are evidence not of a sudden outburst of biblical enthusiasm on the part of some Prussian general, but of an unfortunate chapter in the history of

In the northern district of Lübars, still within West Berlin's city limits, two day-trippers from the urban centre seek a picnic spot at the edge of a field.

Spandau's (intermittent) community of Jews. The town records show that they were driven from their homes in 1510, leaving the 13th- and 14th-Century tombstones in the Jewish cemetery to be used for the construction of living quarters within the citadel.

Three hundred years later, in 1806, Napoleon occupied the citadel and became master of Spandau. Many houses in the town were burned during its liberation from the French in 1813, but half a century afterwards the Spandauers were able to enjoy a pleasant reversal of fate. At the end of the Franco-Prussian War the citadel became a kind of German Fort Knox and was used to store the 120 million marks in gold coins which were collected as part of France's war reparations. Such shared ups and downs have given the Spandauers a strong sense of community; and although the town has been part of Greater Berlin since 1920, its residents continue to think of themselves as different from other Berliners. To this day, they speak of "going to Berlin" when they mean a trip to the Kurfürstendamm, 20 minutes to the east; by "going to town" they mean old Spandau, with its cobbled market streets and narrow alleyways—a provincial community that has never really capitulated to the big city.

To the north of Spandau lies another large tract of public woodland, the Tegeler Forest, part of which skirts the shore of the 1,000-acre Tegelersee. Here, on the edge of the lake, the French garrison in Berlin maintains a services club that is reputed to have the best French chef in town: it is usually filled to capacity with visiting American and British officer-gourmets. *On mange bien ici.* The Tegel airport near by began its life during the Berlin blockade, when it was constructed in three months as a "secondary" airstrip. During the jet age, however, Tegel was found to have many advantages over the older and more crowded Tempelhof field. The luxurious new Tegel airport, designed to handle five million passengers a year, was opened in 1975, and is now West Berlin's only civil airport (although Tempelhof is kept open for emergencies and military flights).

Not far from the main airport is West Berlin's main river port, the Westhafen, where you can meet people who are river nomads; their lives are spent sailing to the North Sea and back again. Their barges carry whole families—wives, children, dogs, cats—as well as fully a quarter of all the cargo imported into West Berlin. (As a way of life it has lost much of its erstwhile gypsy charm; DDR river police impose stringent security regulations during the day and a half it takes the barges to traverse East Germany.)

To the south, on the far side of the Grunewald, lies the seemingly innocuous green-belt suburb of Dahlem. The neighbourhood U-Bahn station in Dahlem is camouflaged as a half-timbered farmhouse, with a genuine thatched roof. Do you know of a thatched subway station anywhere else in the world? But Dahlem only pretends to be a Hampstead Garden Suburb or Forest Hills Gardens. In reality, it is a sort of Ali Baba's Cave. If you keep

The massive red-brick edifice of Spandau Prison in West Berlin was built in 1876 as a military detention centre for 500 prisoners. After the Second World War, seven of the Nazi leaders sentenced at Nuremburg became its only inhabitants—the last remaining prisoner, Rudolf Hess, costing the Berlin city government more than $400,000 a year to keep.

on walking, past the pretty villas with their immaculate gardens, you will arrive at a rather nondescript collection of buildings that might be mistaken for a high school or a hospital. It is, in fact, one of the most extraordinary treasure-trove museums in the world—and I say this as an old museum buff.

In spite of its modest exterior, Dahlem Museum confronts you with an embarrassment of riches. Where to begin? The picture collection is small but breathtaking. Here are seven of Dürer's finest works and a collection of magnificent Holbeins; masterpieces by Lucas Cranach, Martin Schongauer and Hans Baldung; by Jan Van Eyck and Rogier van der Weyden; by Mategna, Filippo Lippi and Verrochio; seven superb Botticellis and five Raphaels; Titians, Breughels, Vermeers—to say nothing of 26 Rembrandts, including the *Man with the Golden Helmet* and the 1643 *Portrait of Saskia.* The sculptures are no less important: Riemenschneiders and Donatellos, Della Robbias and Vischers, as well as one of the greatest collections of Gothic and Renaissance Madonnas.

The newest wing of the Dahlem Museum holds the ethnographic exhibits. You would have to go to the great Museum of Anthropology in Mexico City to find a more stunning collection of pre-Columbian sculptures, and the Peruvian pottery is unequalled outside Peru. The South Sea Islands section next to it is unique—no other museum of primitive art anywhere in the world has been built on so vast a scale or endowed with such a wealth of materials. Here are not only masks and totems but a whole roomful of Pacific outrigger canoes under full sail—an inspiring sight. There are also whole long-houses thatched with original palm fronds. Some brilliant Berlin ethnographer—in the days when Germany still had Pacific possessions—hit on the idea of dismantling a series of representative South Sea structures and shipping them back home, just as John D. Rockefeller Jr. used to buy monasteries in the South of France to be taken apart stone by stone and reassembled in Fort Tryon Park, New York.

It is not altogether inappropriate that the Freie Universität (Free University) should have its scattered campus virtually on the doorstep of a great collection of dance masks and ceremonial objects: the "FU" has its own set of tribal rituals and, on the face of it, they are not much easier for the outsider to understand than those of the headhunters of New Guinea. A visitor from a more conventional town might assume that here in West Berlin, at a university founded in 1948 by refugees from the communist East, in a city that lives precariously in the shadow of the Wall, the student communist movement might have a difficult time of it. In that assumption, however, our visitor would be grossly mistaken. There is no shortage of student radicals in West Berlin, and the FU is justly famous for its meetings and marches and protests and demonstrations, its red banners and slogans scrawled on walls with capitalist spray paint, and long committee sessions at which everybody loses his temper because it is not clear which are the revisionists and which the Left-wing deviationists.

"It's not really surprising that the Free University became a Mecca for the radicals and the anarchists in the Sixties and early Seventies," explains a young lecturer who has been at the university for the better part of a decade. "First of all, some of the people who fled from the East and enrolled at the university when it was first established came here not because the DDR was communist but because it was not communist enough for them—not idealistic enough, if you follow me. They were Marxists, but in their eyes the DDR was a *Beamtenstaat*—a state run by petty officials instead of by the people. So they came over to West Berlin in order to be free to agitate for the kind of communism they had in mind—beautiful reformist dreams (but no drugs, please).

"They were joined, in due course, by an influx of radical students from West Germany. West Berlin is still under Allied occupation, and hence is a demilitarized city as far as the Germans are concerned. The Bundeswehr (West German Army) is not permitted in the city, and conscription doesn't apply here either. So all the West German pacifists and anti-war protesters made straight for West Berlin, where they could avoid having to serve in the army, and where the intellectual climate (especially during the Vietnam years) was perfectly suited to the kind of agitation that kept making headlines in the world Press. For a while it seemed to the students that the millennium must be just around the corner. Everything was going to be beautiful, egalitarian, non-sexist, you name it.

"But then a certain realism entered the picture, and we began to have doubts. In my own case it started when the student commune in which I lived decided that the grocer on the corner was a capitalist exploiter who should be taken over by the commune. We went to him with our non-negotiable demands. Since all his business was with the students, we thought we could force him out of business if he didn't comply with our ultimatum. He was not at all upset by our visit—showed us his books, which revealed that he was making a very small profit on quite a substantial investment of both time and money.

"He said he'd be happy to go on running the shop if the commune would finance it and guarantee him an annual salary. We thought it over, realized that it was much more than we could hope to do, and were quite content to let him carry on as before. We didn't want the trouble of being unexploited, you see. Gradually we became aware that quite a lot of what we wanted was equally unrealistic. And now, frankly, there are a lot of doubts, where before all we had was certainties."

My friend took me with him to a smoke-filled student *Kneipe* to hear FU students discuss the text of a proposed leaflet dealing with the burning issues of the day. Eleven members were present: eleven voices raised in heated discussion, exhortation, indignation, during a thoroughgoing cross-ventilation of such problems as "Multinational Corporations", "the Shah of Iran", "Intensification of Political Education among the Uncon-

The horizontal swathe of the Wall separates privately owned farmland and homes in rural West Berlin (foreground) from an East German collective farm.

verted", "Agitprop Rock Music for the Cause", "Ultimatum to the City Council about Rubbish Collection", "Three-Room Apartment needed for Six-Man Commune", and "Use of Propane Gas for Molotov Cocktails". This kind of Berlin student talk-in is known colloquially as *hochschulpolitische Auseinandersetzungen*, or "student political confrontations".

Such confrontations are by now an accepted feature of the spring and autumn rites in Dahlem, and are taken in good grace by the university's well-fed, well-housed bourgeois neighbours who remember what it was like to be young and politically active. The phenomenon was regarded less indulgently, perhaps, by some of the old-style liberal professors who were shouted down in their classrooms. On handing in their resignations, some of them could not refrain from pointing out that the "anti-fascism" of the Left-wing extremists bore an uncanny resemblance to the "anti-communism" of the pre-war Nazis, who came to class wearing brown shirts. Was there to be no end to this shouting in chorus for the sake of political conformity? Meanwhile, the bulk of the university's students—more than 30,000 at last count—grind bravely on, cramming for exams and hoping that somebody will have a job for them after graduation. Otherwise there may be a revolution after all.

A few blocks away, also within easy walking distance of the museum, is another of Dahlem's major institutions, the "campus" of the U.S. Army's Berlin Command: PX, snack-bar, movie theatre, and all the comforts of a housing development known as *Klein Amerika* (Little America). The commanding general makes his headquarters in the former Luftgaukommando (Regional Air Command) building, a relatively minor manifestation of Goering's penchant for offices with marble floors. The structure served the Luftwaffe for about eight years and has been occupied by the Americans for more than 30. Their job, essentially, is just to be there, and to be seen to be there; even their wives and children (often more visible than the soldiers themselves) somehow weigh in the balance. Militarily the British, French and American forces in Berlin constitute not much more than a token force—fewer than 12,000 men. They are not a serious impediment to the 16 Soviet divisions said to encircle the city, but enough to make a respectable parade annually on Allied Forces Day (May 12), and to serve as a trip-wire in the event of hostilities.

This is the last "occupied" city in the Western world, and a good deal of pomp and circumstance arises from this curious arrangement. At the annual Bastille Day Ball given by the French commander, with the British officers in their resplendent red dress uniforms and the Americans in their dress blues, one gets the impression that what is being played here is an epilogue to the Congress of Vienna—and perhaps it is.

Not that the garrisons don't take their job seriously: even in sub-zero weather you see the Americans in their open Jeeps, with Arctic parkas and

In Heiligensee village on the shore of the River Havel in northern West Berlin, a fisherman prepares his catch of eels for sale. Havel eels are a traditional Berlin speciality, and anglers along the miles of river banks and the thousand bridges in the city, both East and West, have little difficulty in selling their catches.

frozen faces, making the interminable rounds of the "Wall patrol". This is also the only city in the West where it is not at all unusual to see a tank rolling down the street in the middle of ordinary traffic—and then stop for a red traffic light. One U.S. training area is located right at the Wall in Lichterfelde, south of Dahlem, in full view of the DDR guard towers, a piece of wasteland where infantrymen are taught the art of house-to-house fighting. Sometimes, during the winter, they have been known to toss snowballs over the Wall, though needless to say the practice is frowned on in that tinderbox atmosphere.

Perhaps the most extraordinary thing about Berlin is that none of this is considered in any way extraordinary. "There is so much life in Berlin one doesn't notice the absurdities," says a German editor I know who came here from Munich during the Sixties. "We're unafraid of the paradoxes of our situation. What matters is that we can try out ways of living and thinking that have not really been tried in more conventional places. We have something the Italians call the *arte dell'arrangiarsi*, the art of arranging things for oneself under difficult circumstances." Like most Berliners, he feels that the very limitations of the city help to keep it alive. "One of our writers calls West Berlin *der unbequemste Ort Deutschlands*, the most uncomfortable place in Germany, and that is precisely why so many of them like to live here. We enjoy the fact that there are no simple solutions and no easy formulas."

Cool heads in both East and West Berlin still believe that one day the city will be able to work out a new *modus vivendi*—without the Wall. The city planners, as opposed to the political planners, go on considering Berlin a single organism. When Gropius and his associates laid out the "Gropius city" after the war, they planned the U-Bahn and the autobahn in such a way that one day they could be extended to the DDR's Schönefeld airport, which lies just beyond the Wall. Other architects, too, continue to think about an eventual reunion of the city, and to plan new streets so that they might fit into a single overall concept.

"This was where the post-war world split apart," says my editor friend from Munich. "Perhaps this is also the place where it can begin to be healed. I sometimes think that Berlin was fated to lose its status as a national capital, a *Hauptstadt*, so that it could become an international city, a *Weltstadt*, a city open to the world."

The Life That Was

Silk-hatted spectators watch two duellists test their aristocratic skills in this 1897 photograph taken in Friedenau, then a suburban "villa-colony" of Berlin.

Berlin at the turn of the century, described by Baedeker's guidebook as "the greatest purely modern city in Europe", presented an image of sober solidity and self-satisfaction. Although Social Democrat politicians were already winning support amongst the vastly increased proletariat, few signs of change were yet visible on the remorselessly conventional surface. The Berlin in these pictures, capital of the recently unified German state, was a city where canons of public taste were dictated by the ultra-conservative Kaiser and where the exacting standards of an aristocratic officer caste were obediently accepted by a thriving bourgeoisie. But for all its stultifying conformity, the city exuded an air of permanence and stability that the rest of Europe found impressive. Few suspected how soon the grandiose edifice would collapse.

A copper statue of "Berolina", erected in 1895 to symbolize the Berlin woman, presides over horse-drawn traffic and strolling pedestrians on the Alexanderplatz (left) at the turn of the century. In the background is the Grand Hotel, popular with German businessmen who came to wheel and deal in booming Berlin.

Bicyclists and pedestrians compete with trams, carriages and wagons on the Leipzigerstrasse (above) in the 1890s. The Leipzigerstrasse had once been a quiet residential thoroughfare; but with the city's increasing prosperity, it was transformed into a fashionable avenue of expensive shops, hotels and restaurants.

Officers of the Berlin garrison (right) assume the correct martial stance for a group photograph taken in 1897. The oppressively florid décor of the officers' mess makes a dramatic contrast with the bare floor and plain wooden tables.

Customers and waiters in a suburban beer garden at Treptow (below) stiffen their backs for the benefit of the camera. Open-air beer gardens—a characteristic Berlin institution— were favourite places for organized outings.

80/

Watched by a young female admirer, soldiers of the Berlin garrison demonstrate their aquatic skills (right)—many of them preferring to keep on the caps that identify them as members of the Kaiser's army. The signs forbid them to wash towels in the pool or spit in it.

The photograph above immortalizes wrestling enthusiasts of about 1897, stagily posed on the sandy floor of their backroom gymnasium. Wrestling provided an opportunity to show off manly virtues, and clubs devoted to the sport flourished in Berlin at the turn of the century.

In their snowy flounced caps and petticoats
a group of nannies (left) gossip over their
perambulators in the Tiergarten in 1901. Most
nursemaids were country girls from surrounding
districts who came to Berlin to find work.

A winter morning's skating on the Neuer See in
the Tiergarten (below) was one of the mild and
orderly pleasures enjoyed by Berliners of
the 1890s, here fully accoutred in hats, muffs,
sweeping skirts and tightly buttoned coats.

A state occasion early this century brings out the crowds in front of the Reichstag building, erected in 1884-94 to house the parliament of a united Germany.

4

The True Berliner

West Berliners cheered U.S. President John F. Kennedy when he came to the city in 1963 and delivered his famous four-word pronunciamento: "*Ich bin ein Berliner!*" (I am a Berliner!) At that moment he could have been elected mayor of Berlin by a landslide. But what, indeed, *is* a Berliner—not as a political symbol, but in the flesh; the genuine article—*ein echter Berliner?* An easy way to meet the true Berliner is to go on a hot summer day to Tegel, the Wannsee or one of the other stretches of water that dot the western edge of the city.

There you will find the male of the species—casually clad or near naked, young or old, tall or short, skinny or bulky, relaxed or intense, but talking, talking, for ever talking: about this year's holiday and last year's, the inflated price of everything, the troubles he is having with his wife and/or girl friend, his chances of a tax rebate, the latest Yugoslav or Polish film sensation. There, too, is the equally talkative female of the species who typically, in my subjective view, is lithe, frank, impertinent and more often than not very pretty indeed.

Berliners talk and gesticulate as animatedly as Romans or Milanese and their attention span is correspondingly short. They think, talk and move as if they haven't got a minute to lose. All these traits are vestigial, I think, left over from the days when bustling Berlin was the sixth largest city in the world, not way down the list as it is today. There is no good reason now, what with comfortable working hours and long weekends, why Berliners should be in such a hurry to get where they are going. Yet they are. I have seen a crowd of impatient pedestrians surging across a busy West Berlin street, not only against the lights—an unthinkable act in any other German city—but also against the upraised hand of a traffic policeman.

So much talking and rushing about is thirsty work, requiring a frequent intake of beer or *Himbeer* (raspberry) lemonade. Sometimes the lubricant is an improbable combination called *Berliner Weisse mit Schuss* (Berlin white beer with a dash of raspberry syrup), which is highly recommended as a cheap substitute for champagne. The waiter pours a large dollop of ruby-red syrup into the bottom of a hefty glass and then decants a bottle of yeasty white beer into it. The mixture foams, it bubbles, it plays a sinfonietta in pink and white, shamelessly tickling the end of your nose. But the true Berliner will continue to talk throughout this performance, desisting only when the glass is already at his lips and his nose disappears into the foam.

Berliners are great talkers because they feel the need to communicate. Not for them the tribal beer-drinking habits of their inarticulate cousins in

A widow in East Berlin smiles broadly during a pause in her carpet beating. Like many others of her generation, she has lost loved ones in two world wars and endured the destruction and division of her city, but manages to retain the tough stoicism of the true Berliner.

south Germany, who will sit, 80 or 100 young men in identical white shirts, banging 80 or 100 steins of beer on the tables in four-four rhythm while an all-girl brass band blares out old army marches from a near-by bandstand. Who can get a word in edgeways amid that racket? Besides, the music is enough to cause indigestion. There are places like that in Berlin, but they are for tourists. Berliners prefer places where they can talk to one another.

The language, of course, is *Berlinerisch*, the pass key to a club, a secret dialect, like Swiss-German, that other Germans cannot relate to and do not care to hear. This is one of the reasons why West Germans are not overly fond of visiting Berlin: they feel snubbed. Not that the Berliners are un-friendly; they simply prefer to express themselves in their own verbal short-hand rather than go to the trouble of speaking "High" German.

In Berlin it is easier to be a stranger from another country, because the natives make an effort to communicate with you in their best high school English or French, and you will never understand why tourists from Frankfurt complain that Berliners are unapproachable. The fact is, with rare exceptions you do not need an introduction to talk to them—usually they will approach you first. The conventional Berlin opening line is a short, incisive quip that takes in the state of the world and indicates the speaker's philosophical approach to it, preferably in two words or less.

I remember how one day, at a lakeside beach or *Strandbad*, I stood wrestling with a recalcitrant vending machine that had swallowed my D-mark without coughing up a chocolate bar. A gorgeous Berlin brunette stepped up to me, took in my feckless efforts with a sympathetic glance, and murmured: *"Tückisch, was?"*, a phrase whose full import, as closely as I can approximate it, was: "Life is full of traps; and that wretched, sneaky piece of machinery is a typical example. You have my wholehearted sympathies in your sisyphean endeavours."

Such a typical Berlin introduction can lead to a friendly counterploy, an invitation to have a cup of coffee or share a curry sausage at the nearest Imbiss stand. An Imbiss, I should mention, is ideally suited to the hectic needs of the Berliners, affording them not only quick and inexpensive nourishment, but also an opportunity to talk at any hour of the day or night. While the proprietor lays the sausages in a cooking device that resembles the apparatus used by dentists to sterilize their instruments, he invariably delivers a running commentary on the weather, the latest international crisis, the football results and other vital topics.

Once you've met your true Berliner, she—or he—will soon treat you to a taste of the famous local *Mutterwitz*, or mother wit. It may be expressed in the form of a pun, quip, anecdote or extempore joke, but it is bound to be acerbic and may well be downright outrageous. A typical example that first went the rounds of Berlin at the turn of the century involved one of the city's bankers, who was asked: "Did you hear who died this morning?" "No," the banker replied, "but anyone is all right with me."

Glasses stand temporarily neglected as two habitués of West Berlin's oldest Kneipe, which dates from 1877, argue a point. Although this establishment is famed for its selection of house-bottled wines, its patrons—being Berliners—come to talk as much as to drink.

This *Mutterwitz* is directed most effectively against those in authority. In 1933, when the aged President Paul von Hindenburg was inveigled into affixing his signature to the document naming Adolf Hitler Chancellor, the Berliners joked that the Wilhelmstrasse should now be swept twice a day since Hindenburg was likely to sign any scrap of paper that blew his way. In 1945, when Soviet troops laid siege to the city, propaganda Minister Joseph Goebbels' last-ditch assurances of ultimate German victory were greeted with the comment: "Of course we're bound to win—especially now that we can travel all the way from the Eastern to the Western front by subway."

A favourite Berlin story during the early days of the four-power occupation concerned a character named Patschke, from East Berlin, who ran into his friend, Krause, from the West. "You people in the West," Patschke tells him, "are all being exploited by the capitalists. You don't know anything about working-class solidarity. Did you know that we're on such good terms with the Russians that they even insist on driving us home from work in their army trucks?"

"That's nothing," Krause replies. "On our side an American officer will stop his big car and invite you to come back home to his villa. And then you get champagne, and can drink and smoke all you like. Afterwards you can even take a bath in his tub."

"That's just propaganda," says Patschke indignantly. "Do you mean to tell me all this has already happened to you?"

"Not to me," Krause concedes, "but to my sister."

Cynical, irreverent and often grimly sardonic, the wisecrack is the Ber-

Although many West Berliners have plots of
land in one of the city's multiple "garden
colonies", few have gardens attached to their
homes. This woman is luckier than most.
Her home has a large garden that she has
tended for many years, embellishing it with
a miniature house and a tribe of gnomes.

liners' equivalent of whistling in the dark—and over the past 500 years there has been plenty of dark for them to whistle in.

When the Hohenzollerns, a family of ambitious noblemen from southern Germany, acquired the overlordship of Brandenburg in 1415, Berlin, the province's market town, was small but prosperous and independent, running its own affairs in alliance with the powerful city-states of the Hanseatic League, which also included Hamburg and Bremen.

The Berliners were determined to retain their sovereignty, but in 1442 the second Hohenzollern ruler, Friedrich "Irontooth" (so-called because he never yielded what he once got his teeth into) took advantage of a dispute between the powerful craft guilds and the patrician families to gain control of the city. Forced to sever its ties with the Hanseatic League and deprived of its right to self-government, Berlin was no longer to be an independent township, but a princely capital, a *Residenzstadt*.

A heavily fortified castle, representing Hohenzollern domination, was built within the city walls on a tract of land extorted from the municipality, and "Irontooth" settled down to show the Berliners who was boss. His harshness, however, goaded them into rebellion and 600 armoured knights had to be summoned into the city to restore his authority. The insurrection was recorded by contemporary chroniclers as an example of *Berliner Unwille*—the Berliners' unwillingness to follow orders—and this attitude has characterized much of their subsequent history.

"Irontooth" marked his victory over the city by forcing it to adopt a new and humiliating coat of arms. Berlin's heraldic bear—until then a rampant and rather ferocious creature—was dropped on all fours and given a chain collar; on its back was perched the heraldic eagle of the Hohenzollerns. The new device was singularly apt, for it symbolized precisely the uneasy relationship between the shackled but still far from tamed Berliners and their authoritarian rulers. (When military defeat and revolutionary upheaval forced Kaiser Wilhelm II's abdication in 1918, the eagle was banished from the city emblem and the bear resumed an upright position, losing its iron collar in the process. Although Germany was now a republic, above the liberated bear was placed a five-pointed crown, a reminder of Berlin's continuing claim to be an "imperial" city.)

Prussia's "Iron Chancellor", Otto von Bismarck, who united all of Germany under Hohenzollern rule in 1871, was always grumbling about *Berliner Unwille*. He was irritated by the fact that the city consistently voted for liberal Reichstag deputies and not for his candidates. At one stage he even considered moving the Reichstag to another city in the hope that Berlin's always baulky representatives might attend less frequently.

The Nazis were equally put out by the Berliners' obstinate reluctance to travel in any direction but the one they chose for themselves. Even on the eve of his accession to power, Hitler was unable to win more than a third of their votes; and in the municipal elections of March, 1934, with the Nazis

The modern generation of West Berliners have created their own favourite in-places, such as this leafy self-service beer garden off the busy Kurfürstendamm.

actually in charge, the recalcitrant Berliners insisted on casting a majority of votes for the Nazis' opponents. The distaste that many a true Berliner felt for Hitler and his brownshirted hooligans was expressed with succinct and characteristic asperity by Max Liebermann, the deposed president of the Prussian Academy of Art. Looking out of his Berlin studio window one day at a procession of Nazi Stormtroopers, Liebermann turned to his companion and remarked: "Pity one can't eat as much as one wants to puke."

It may seem paradoxical that a people who have enjoyed only relatively few years of freedom throughout their history should have become notorious for their dissenting tradition. But, like New York, Berlin has always been a city of immigrants and its continual exposure to new ideas and impulses has helped to counterbalance the constraints of authoritarian rule. It has few inhibitions about strangers—why should it when, for more than 100 years, native-born Berliners have never accounted for as much as 50 per cent of the population? Indeed, many of those whose names symbolize "Berlin" to the rest of the world—Günter Grass, for example, or Willy Brandt, Bertolt Brecht and Heinrich Zille—became Berliners only by adoption.

The true Berliner may be descended not only from natives of the surrounding province of Brandenburg (few of them are), but also from Danes, French, Thuringians, Silesians, Saxons, Dutch, Slavs, Italians, Waldensians, Jews. . . . In the 1870s one investigator into the ancestry of the Berliner estimated that little more than 37 per cent of the city's population were of "German" descent. He reckoned that some 39 per cent were "Latins"— mainly French, Belgian and Italian—and the remainder of Slavic origin. At best this was only an educated guess; and the mixture has changed considerably since then, especially in the years following the Second World War, when Turks, Greeks, Yugoslavs, Arabs, Spaniards and other "guest workers" poured into the Western half of the city.

This melting-pot tradition, interrupted only by the racism of the Hitler years, has its roots in the geography of Berlin. The city rises out of what used to be known as "the sand-box of the Holy Roman Empire". Geologically, this area was once an ocean-bed, botanically little more than a desert. When they dig foundations in Berlin, the steam shovels bring up nothing but the purest golden sand, of the kind that travel agents promise you at Mikonos or Djerba. Centuries of dogged cultivation have added a layer of topsoil in many places, but to the north of the city vast tracts are still as desolate as they were in the Middle Ages when almost the whole of Brandenburg consisted of marshes, lakes, moors, and forests of birch and pine.

As a border territory between eastern and western Europe, however, Brandenburg offered enormous strategic potential. Indeed, Berlin achieved its prosperity by providing a vital link in the network of trade routes that led from upland towns like Meissen and Dresden to the Baltic coast, and from Magdeburg to Cracow and the territories of Russia. In order

Symbol of the City

In Berlin—both East and West—the city's traditional heraldic emblem of a rampant bear remains prominent. In the West it is the central figure of the city seal and is worn by policemen (centre row, right), firemen (bottom row, left) and even troops of the Western powers (centre row, left). In the East, the bear can be seen playing a more informal role, hefting pretzels on bakery signs (top row), or encouraging tots to keep their city free of litter (bottom row, right).

But the Berlin *Bär* has not always enjoyed such supremacy. For most of the city's history the bear has been rivalled or dominated by the eagle—a common emblem of authority. The changing relationship of bear to eagle—often a reflection of the uneasy relationship between Berlin and its rulers—is depicted on the cover of a Nazi booklet (above), printed in 1937 to commemorate the city's 700th anniversary. In 1280, for example, bears were given equal billing with the eagle of the Margraves of Brandenburg, who granted the city a privileged status as a trade centre. But by 1450 the bear was chained, with the Hohenzollern eagle perched on its back. In 1937, the Hitler regime allowed the bear to appear unaccompanied by the Nazi eagle—no doubt they were trying to flatter the Berliners—and the bear has stood alone ever since.

fully to exploit the potential of their territory—to which was added the sparsely populated province of East Prussia at the beginning of the 17th Century—the Hohenzollerns needed soldiers, settlers, craftsmen and traders. Such people were in short supply and the rulers of Brandenburg-Prussia were prepared to welcome them from almost anywhere.

In 1685, Friedrich Wilhelm, known as "the Great Elector" on account of his triumphs on the battlefield, invited thousands of Huguenots—Protestant refugees who had been expelled from France—to settle on his lands. Many moved to Berlin and, by 1688, 20 of every 100 Berliners were of French origin. The newcomers brought with them sophisticated technologies—such as watchmaking, enamelling, glove manufacture and silk-weaving—that formed the basis for a much more luxurious life-style than the native-born Brandenburgers had been accustomed to. Having set up the brewing of *Berliner Weisse*, the Huguenots also introduced the city's first public means of transportation—sedan chairs. They influenced the language as well as the life-style of the Berliners and many French words were incorporated into *Berlinerisch* argot. A charming example of *Berlinerisch* pidgin French is the word, *Amusmang*, which is still used by Berliners to describe their traditional weekend trips to the lakes and woods surrounding the city.

Not everyone was pleased by the foreign influence. "Today everything has to be French," one native-born Berliner noted sourly in 1689. "You cannot even hope to be received at court any more if you do not speak French! Children four or five years old, even those just barely able to crawl, are being introduced to French gallantries. Let a young man hope to succeed with a girl, then he must appear wearing French hats, waistcoats and silk stockings. No one cares if he has crooked legs, calf's eyes, a buzzard's beak, buck teeth—no matter, so long as he behaves French."

In his desire to build up the population, the Great Elector was prepared to welcome not only Protestants and Catholics, but also Jews. A small colony of Jews lived in Berlin as early as the 13th Century, but when the plague came in the 1340s they were blamed for having brought it to Berlin, and from then on they were the potential scapegoats for every disaster. Like Jews elsewhere in Europe, those of Berlin were forever liable to persecution and expulsion, and in 1573 they were driven from the city "for all eternity". In 1671, however, the Great Elector decided that an expanding population was more important than an ancient prejudice, and Jews were permitted to return to Berlin.

Two generations later, when Prussia had become a kingdom, Friedrich Wilhelm I (1713-40), faced the problem not only of adding to his population but of keeping the one he already had. A rotund, choleric and red-faced man who quickly became known as "the Drill-Sergeant", Friedrich Wilhelm was determined to turn his nation into a major military power. For this he needed revenue as well as recruits, and Berlin was ordered to provide both. The city's merchants were taxed to the hilt and its able-bodied

Late 19th-Century apartment blocks huddled around courtyards in central West Berlin demonstrate how the burgeoning capital was able to absorb the million immigrant workers who helped to quadruple its population between 1850 and the turn of the century.

citizens became prey for military press-gangs. The king also decreed that all new houses were to have attic rooms in which troops could be billeted; and his architects laid out wide streets, including the Friedrichstrasse and the Wilhelmstrasse, that lent themselves to grandiose military parades. Such measures enabled Friedrich Wilhelm to build up his army, but they also turned Berlin into a giant barracks from which many preferred to flee.

The king's solution, like the problem itself, was curiously prophetic. To prevent escapes, and as an aid to tax-collecting, he had a high wall built around the city. Thus, the first Berlin wall designed to keep people in rather than out was built, not as is generally supposed, by East Germany's communist boss, Walter Ulbricht, in 1961, but by Friedrich Wilhelm in 1735.

The inward flow to Berlin resumed under the Drill-Sergeant's son, Frederick the Great (1740-1786). "And if Turks and pagans would come here to populate this land," he declared at the beginning of his reign, "I would build mosques and temples for them." (The Turks of modern-day Kreuzberg, incidentally, still have no mosque in their district.) Frederick was no less ambitious—or ruthless—than his father; but unlike Friedrich Wilhelm, the new king was also concerned with style and elegance, and under his energetic and pervasive influence the cultural atmosphere of Berlin became emphatically cosmopolitan.

In the ensuing decades Berlin grew into one of the great intellectual centres of Germany. As the young Romantic movement in the city gathered momentum a spate of writers and scholars migrated to the Prussian capital, especially after Wilhelm von Humboldt established the University of Berlin in 1810. The city's reputation for artistic and literary excellence was created by Ludwig Tieck, Friedrich Schlegel, E. T. A. Hoffmann, Adelbert von Chamisso, Friedrich Hegel, Felix Mendelssohn, Achim von Arnim and a dozen others who gave it an intellectual radiance it had never known before.

At the same time, Unter den Linden emerged as a fashionable boulevard crowded with poets, students, officers, beautiful women, painters and musicians. It was "a world of elegance", according to the poet Heinrich Heine, who published his first love lyrics in Berlin during the 1820s. "What a polished crowd surges up and down these 'Linden'! See that dandy with his many gaily coloured waistcoats? Hear him whispering earnest words to his lady? He ogles her through his lorgnette, smiles, fusses his hair. What beautiful women one sees and what a lot of men glittering with medals! Those countless decorations everywhere! Have a coat fitted here, and your tailor asks immediately, 'With or without a notch for the ribbons?'"

Yet, in spite of the mannered grace of the city's *haute-monde*, the average Berliner retained the cocky and abrasive good humour that Goethe had noted during the final years of Frederick the Great's reign: "I see in everything that this is a city filled with such an impertinent species of mankind," he wrote, "that one doesn't get far using delicacy with them; to keep above water in Berlin, one has to be somewhat coarse oneself."

A City Forged in Conflict

911	Germanic tribal duchies of Bavaria, Swabia, Thuringia, Franconia, Frisia, Saxony and Lorraine elect Duke Conrad of Franconia King of Germans
962	The Pope summons Otto, King of Germans, to Rome as papal protector and crowns him King of Romans, thus laying basis for what evolved into Holy Roman Empire of the German Nation, lasting until 1806
1134-57	Albrecht the Bear, Saxon nobleman, extends Germany's north-eastern borders by conquering Slavonic territory of Brandenburg. German settlers move into region, establishing small fishing town of Berlin on banks of River Spree
1230-42	The Margrave (ruler) of Brandenburg grants charter to Berlin; it, together with sister town of Cölln, on an island in the Spree, grows as trading centre
1307	Berlin and Cölln set up common town council and join Hanseatic League, powerful trading association of north German city-states
1391	Preoccupied with the feuds and intrigues of his noblemen, the Margrave of Brandenburg allows the two towns to become virtually self-governing. They set up joint court of justice
1415	As reward for helping him gain the imperial crown, Holy Roman Emperor Sigismund invests Friedrich von Hohenzollern, a nobleman from Nuremburg in South Germany, with newly created electorship of Brandenburg. This dignity entitles Friedrich and his heirs to cast a vote, with six other German peers, whenever a Holy Roman Emperor is to be chosen
1442	Elector Friedrich II, known as "Irontooth", asserts Hohenzollern authority over Berlin and Cölln, abolishing many privileges and forcing them to sever ties with the Hanseatic League
1448	"Irontooth" suppresses revolt led by Berliners; both towns are absorbed into the state of Brandenburg
1486	Berlin becomes official residence of the Hohenzollerns
1539	The Reformation engulfs Germany. Brandenburg becomes one of the "protesting states" when its ruler embraces Lutheranism
1555	Peace of Augsburg seeks to resolve religious conflict within Holy Roman Empire. Lutheran and Catholic princes of Germany promise not to make war against one another
1614-18	During Thirty Years' War between the Catholic and Protestant states of Europe, Berlin is destroyed
1618	Duke of Prussia dies without male heirs; title and territory pass to his son-in-law, Elector Johann Sigismund of Brandenburg. Although Prussia lies many miles north-east of Brandenburg on coast of Baltic Sea, the two territories form core of the future Prussian kingdom
1640-88	Friedrich Wilhelm of Brandenburg, known as "the Great Elector", rebuilds Berlin and brings in Dutch hydraulic specialists to construct network of barge canals, quays and arched bridges
1685	Thousands of Protestant Huguenots, expelled from France, settle in Berlin
1701	Prussia and Brandenburg become joint Kingdom of Prussia
1709	Berlin and Cölln finally unite as one city
1713-14	Friedrich Wilhelm I, nicknamed "the Drill-Sergeant", establishes Prussian tradition of militarism; builds wall round Berlin to prevent disenchanted citizens from escaping
1740-86	Realizing Prussian strength depends upon an expanding population, Frederick the Great encourages massive immigration from France, Flanders, Bohemia and Switzerland as well as other parts of Germany. Many newcomers flock to Berlin, giving city increasingly cosmopolitan atmosphere
1756-63	Seven Years' War between Anglo-Prussian alliance and coalition of Austria, Saxony, France and Russia ends with Prussia's emergence as a great power
1791	Completion of 65-foot-high Brandenburg Gate by the neo-classical architect Carl Gotthard Langhans

During the 18th Century Berlin's population grew from 90,000 to 150,000. In the next 100 years the rate of expansion increased even more dramatically as the city's burgeoning industries attracted workers from every corner of Germany and Europe. The increase was particularly spectacular after 1871, when the capital of the newly proclaimed German Empire became an irresistible magnet to thousands from the provinces. By 1900 the city's population had rocketed from 700,000 to almost two million. "Berlin has become the drainage canal for the provinces," wrote one observer, half in admiration and half in regret. "All that is best and worst in the provinces comes pouring into this place—only the mediocre stay at home." The influx to the city was matched by a rush to the surrounding suburbs, so that when Greater Berlin was established in 1920, the new metropolis had a total of four million inhabitants.

In the 1890s there was an adage, "The true Berliner comes from Breslau". This saying requires an explanation, for you may no longer be able to find Breslau on the map. It has become Wroclaw, in Poland. Once it was the capital of Silesia, a great mining and cloth-weaving province that Frederick the Great wrested from the Austrian Empress Maria Theresia. Silesia was then a beautiful but exploited province, its history being rather like that of Ireland in some respects; and just as the Irish regularly sent their sons to England or the United States, the Silesians sent their sons to Berlin.

One of them was Gerhart Hauptmann, who shook up the city's bourgeois theatre audiences in the 1890s with his powerful dramas of poverty and social injustice. He brought a whole new dimension to the German stage and went on to become one of the grand old men of literature. *Die Weber* (*The Weavers*), the play that made Hauptmann famous throughout Europe, deals with the desperate conditions in the Silesian linen industry that led to the abortive weavers' revolt of 1844. The play (which was banned at first by the Berlin police on the grounds that it was an open incitement to rioting) has always meant a great deal to me, not only because Hauptmann was a friend of my grandfather, but also because it provides an astonishingly vivid picture of the industry to which four generations of my father's family devoted their lives.

The cultivation and manufacture of linen has its own complex history, in Silesia as well as Ireland; suffice it to say that the process is labour intensive and that its workers were often inhumanly exploited. It was always a matter of special pride to the old Grünfelds, however, that their mills had never had a strike. The original F. V. Grünfeld spent much of his time trying to improve the weavers' lot and, among other things, he established the first vocational weaving school for the many crippled and handicapped children of the area.

His descendants continued manufacturing linen in the town of Landeshut, but also expanded into the growing markets of Berlin and western Germany. They established branches in Berlin and Cologne, and moved their head offices, as royal linen-weavers, to the imperial capital. That was how my father came to be a native-born *echter Berliner* with the proverbial ties to the province of Silesia.

Berlin, of course, is not the only city that has depended on immigration for its survival. But what makes it unique, I think, is the extraordinary intensity of feeling it inspires among even the most cosmopolitan of its inhabitants. Bismarck was fond of describing the reaction of a Berliner whom he once took on a tour of the lovely Herrenhausen Palace garden in Hanover. The garden was nothing at all compared to Unter den Linden, said the Berliner. A year later, according to Bismarck, he walked down Unter den Linden with this same Berliner. It was midsummer and hot, and the linden trees had a particularly drab, miserable look about them. But when Bismarck recalled the gorgeous trees at Herrenhausen, his companion exclaimed, "Oh, for heaven's sake, leave me alone! I can't tell you how furious I get when I see something that's better than we've got in Berlin!"

Berliners are not patriotic Germans in the sense that they identify emotionally with the Bonn Federal Republic, the DDR or the erstwhile Reich; but they have a proprietary feeling towards their city, a sense of communal pride that I have rarely encountered elsewhere (the inhabitants

In the 1930s Berlin was often the scene of spectacles such as this in which searchlights, piercing the sky for several miles above Hitler's Olympic Stadium, formed a pyramid (below) and an hourglass (below right). The displays were conceived by Hitler's official architect for Berlin, Albert Speer. The one shown here marked Mussolini's visit to the Nazi capital in 1937. The British Ambassador, Sir Nevile Henderson, commented that "it was like being in a cathedral of ice".

of most big cities seem to take a masochistic pleasure in disparaging their own town). In Berlin the phone booths remain intact, the subway trains have never been smeared with spray paint, as in New York, and people actually stoop in the street to pick up litter dropped by careless strangers.

The modern Berliner's commitment to his city is, I suspect, one of his acquisitions from the school of hard knocks. He has seen the city tyrannized, destroyed, occupied, blockaded and divided; but the thought that everyone who lives here shares its problems and anxieties still acts as a powerful cohesive force, in the East as well as the West. Ironically, it was the Russians who helped to reinforce the morale of West Berliners when they imposed their blockade on the city in June, 1948. No one knew at the outset that it would be possible for the Western Allies to bring in provisions; with only 10 days' supply of coal and about a month's supply of food, West Berliners seemed to face the prospect of starvation or surrender.

But as West Berlin's mayor Ernst Reuter put it, "the risk of cold and hunger is far better than the guarantee of slavery". Sustained by the Western airlift, the Berliners held out against the blockade for almost a year. The spirit in which they met the ordeal was poignantly expressed by the poet

Gottfried Benn. Writing from the beleaguered city to a friend in West Germany at the start of the siege, Benn declared: "And so now I say farewell and ask you to accept these greetings from darkened, blockaded Berlin, and from a part of it, moreover, which is close to starvation. This is being written in a room filled with shadows, in which the electric light has burned for only two out of the past 24 hours, for our gloomy and rain-filled summer has even robbed the city of its last chance at any luck and settled autumn over our ruins, ever since our spring began. Yet this remains the city whose lustre I love; whose misery I now choose to bear with civic pride; whose second, third and now fourth Reich I have experienced, and which nothing could now tempt me into leaving."

The Soviet blockade failed to achieve its objective of forcing the Western Allies out of Berlin. By the time it was lifted, in May, 1949, the Federal Republic had been established, the North Atlantic Alliance had been formed in response to the Russian challenge and the Western Allies had demonstrated their determination to defend their rights in West Berlin. Above all, according to General Lucius Clay, the U.S. military governor in Germany, the city had "regained its soul".

In June, 1953, it was the East Berliners' turn to make headlines. Already under intense pressure to increase industrial productivity, they were ordered to raise their "voluntary" work norms by 10 per cent; they responded, instead, with a massive eruption of *Unwille*. There were strikes, marches and rallies; the Red Flag was torn down from the Brandenburg Gate. Eventually, Soviet troops were sent in to restore order; and while West Berliners stood by, powerless to help, the workers of East Berlin tried to fight tanks with bricks and paving stones. "A man's heart could stop," said Ernst Reuter, "as we see this city murdered by the forces of history in which we have all been torn."

The uprising was quickly suppressed by the Soviet army and Walter Ulbricht's efficient police apparatus, but over the next eight years millions of refugees from the DDR used West Berlin as an escape hatch to the West. The issue was finally resolved, after a fashion, by the construction of the Wall in August, 1961. Hundreds of Berliners had risked their lives to help Jews hide from their Nazi oppressors during the Second World War: now West Berliners began taking similar risks to help friends and relatives escape from behind the Wall.

I know of one West Berlin woman who was caught carrying a letter that contained escape instructions for the brother of a friend. She received a four-year sentence and had to serve nearly two years in a DDR women's prison. When she was finally released, she uttered not a word of reproach against the friends who had involved her in the scheme. She had done her best; it had been the decent thing to do, and she had known the risk. By now it should be apparent that the true Berliner cuts something of a heroic figure: tenacious, long-suffering, reacting to every blow of fate with

A West Berlin traffic policeman wears a white raincoat and a belt of battery-powered flashing lights to make him more visible to motorists and pedestrians. The equipment is meant to give him a better—and safer—chance of controlling the city's aggressive road users.

one of his rueful jokes. Yet the Berliner is not disposed to see himself in heroic terms: on the contrary, he rather resents any effort at mythologizing. "As soon as I begin to praise my good Berliners," wrote the poet Heinrich Heine more than a century-and-a-half ago, "I know my reputation among them is finished. They shrug their shoulders and whisper, 'That fellow's become insipid; now he's even praising us!'"

Even so, I can hardly refrain from giving the true Berliner his due. In the face of every kind of aggravation—political, cultural, psychological—he has managed to retain his sardonic and imperturbable *sang-froid.* No story better illustrates this attitude than the one about a Berlin taxi driver that the U.S. foreign correspondent George Bailey tells in his book, *Germans.* Bailey heard it from Fritz Kortner, the emigré actor and director, who returned to Berlin in 1953 nursing an exile's grudge against the land he had been forced to leave 20 years earlier.

When Kortner arrived at Tempelhof Airport and settled into a cab, he was surprised to hear the driver ask: "Where would you like to go, Mr. Kortner?"

"What, you know who I am?"

"Why, of course, Mr. Kortner. In the old days I used to drive you to the theatre every night."

Slightly mollified, Kortner sat back to enjoy his first look at post-war Berlin. At the next traffic lights the driver turned to him and asked, "Tell me, Mr. Kortner, when did you leave Germany?"

"In 1933, when Hitler came to power."

"And you've only just now come back?"

"That's right."

The driver mulled it over for a while. But when they reached Kortner's hotel he told the actor reassuringly, by way of farewell: "You know, Mr. Kortner—you didn't miss much."

Traces of a Vanished Era

PHOTOGRAPHS BY THOMAS HÖPKER

A stained and eroded skull looks down from a crumbling tomb in the Sophienkirche Cemetery. The cemetery lies almost in the shadow of the Berlin Wall.

As East Berlin, the capital of a new communist Germany, pushes its way confidently into the future, it seems to have left behind without a backward glance the Berlin of the past. Yet, paradoxically, just because the past is ignored so completely, its scattered traces can survive—unregarded, undisturbed, unrestored—with a poignancy and immediacy that would be impossible in a city that took a conscious pride in them.

Saplings grow inside once-fashionable churches; tombs moulder in unvisited cemeteries; forgotten advertisements fade slowly on high, blank walls. Jean Cocteau once noted that the ruins in post-war Berlin "added a profoundly poetic note . . . and introduced a dreamlike quality". In East Berlin some of those ruins have remained almost untouched; and in the city's shadowed corners a hint of that dreamlike quality still lingers.

Near the gaunt, pillared portico of the ruined Deutscher Dom, neo-classical statues recline in the weeds.

Shattered Mementoes of Worship

On East Berlin's Platz der Akademie stand two fine 18th-Century churches, but their windows are blank and their statues lie toppled around them. Although scheduled for eventual restoration by the DDR regime, they have remained virtually untouched since they were burnt out in Second World War air-raids. In their derelict courtyards lingers a breath of the past, long since banished from the reconstructed palaces of near-by Unter den Linden.

In the Französischer Dom—twin of the Deutscher Dom that faces it across the square—green leaves soften a monument battered long ago by wartime shelling.

A stone finial survives intact over the roof beams of the Französischer Dom.

Through the breached roof of the Französischer Dom light pours into its derelict interior. High above rear the columns that carried the once-graceful dome.

Two ageing advertisements—one for coal briquets overlaying another for cigarettes—blur into each other.

Dimmed by time, a burgher proffers his beer-mug, advertising a traditional brew that is still made in Berlin.

Weather-beaten after long exposure, the skilfully painted sign of a cobbler proclaims the careful personal attention he gave to shoes half-a-century ago.

A derelict brewery in Bergstrasse still seems to embody the triumphant commercialism that typified the old Imperial Berlin.

Labelled "Peace" and "Quiet", two pensive angels adorn the entrance to an untended family tomb in the Dorotheenstadt Cemetery.

Tombstones in the large Jewish Cemetery at Weissensee, in the north-eastern suburbs of East Berlin, are almost lost among encroaching trees. The forlorn graves evoke the days of the mid-19th Century when Berlin's flourishing and gifted Jewish community played an influential role in the cultural life of the city.

5

The Other Side of the Wall

In any city you want to see something of its past glories: the Acropolis, the Colosseum, Notre-Dame. Here in Berlin the centre of the pre-war city and its principal relics belong to the East, or as they themselves prefer to call it, "Berlin, capital of the DDR". This coincidence of geography raises some tricky ideological problems, since in the capital of the DDR they pride themselves on having broken with the past. The major monuments of medieval religion, Hohenzollern monarchy and Prussian imperialism are not ideal symbols for the first "workers' and peasants' state" to be established on German soil. But if you are intrigued by the idea of royal palaces converted into people's restaurants and of classical buildings dedicated to heroes of Soviet history, there is much to discover in the East.

To get there you have to submit to a checkpoint procedure that is only slightly less wearisome than a spell in a submarine decompression chamber. I shall reproduce here, by way of description, some jottings I scrawled on the backs of a couple of envelopes during a recent passage by car through the only crossing point for non-Germans, Check Point Charlie, on the Friedrichstrasse:

Notice on board: "You are now leaving the American Sector." U.S., British and French military policemen do not even look up as I drive past. Next sign: "Stop." A DDR border guard waves me up to the barrier, raises the pole, checks my passport, hands out a numbered slip. I run a slalom course around cement barriers, and park in an assigned lot behind the first building. Guards in a watch-tower observe all my movements. I enter the first building and stand in a queue for eight minutes. I hand the slip, my passport and car registration to a churlish guard behind a counter. The documents disappear through a chute into a room behind the guard. I fill out a customs declaration, listing all monies carried. Then I wait with 30 or 40 others for 15 minutes. Most are Turkish migrant workers going over to see East Berlin girl friends; some carry flowers or chocolates.

Our passports are finally handed back to us one at a time by a rude, irritable functionary. He gives me long, searching glances to compare my face with the photograph in my passport. I wait 10 minutes in the next queue, contemplating a large colour reproduction on the wall: A. M. Gerassimov's *Lenin on the Rostrum*, printed in the U.S.S.R. For light relief, there is a poster as well: "Our Republic—honoured, respected, recognized." A young Turkish worker ahead of me in the queue is led off, with a pained expression, to an adjoining room to undergo a body search.

I submit to a personal customs check by an older, overbearing official

Between the historic Brandenburg Gate (foreground) and the ultra-modern East German parliament (background centre) lies the tree-lined avenue of Unter den Linden. Once the main thoroughfare of Berlin, it is now a grandiose dead-end: the Wall (out of the picture) passes a few feet in front of the Gate.

flanked by a courteous young woman, also in uniform. "Anything to declare?" I resist a sudden impulse to click my heels, shoot out my right arm and shout: "I haff nozing to declare but my undying loyalty to ze Führer!" Instead, I give a convincing assurance that I bear no gifts, printed matter or other merchandise. My papers are stamped by the young woman. There is another wait at an exchange counter in an adjoining building, then an additional eight minutes outside a third building for a car check. A brusque guard examines my passport, papers, then car: he dips into the side pockets, folds the seats forward, fumbles in the dashboard compartment looking for newspapers, magazines, books. I have carefully cleaned out the car in anticipation. (Once I had to stand half-an-hour in freezing cold while an old newspaper I had inadvertently left in my car was "examined"—read?—inside the guardhouse, then confiscated.) I get a nod of approval and am permitted to drive on.

I proceed to the final barrier pole. A guard checks my papers; once again my face is compared with the photograph in my passport. The pole is lifted; at last I drive out along the Friedrichstrasse.

Once safely in East Berlin—you could have come just as well but no more easily by underground or elevated train to the Friedrichstrasse station, or through Check Point Charlie on foot—you will find that you have literally arrived in a new era. Even time is reckoned differently on this side of the city. If you visit the Pergamon Museum, for example, with its world-famous collection of Greek and Near-Eastern antiquities, you will notice that the museum guides and labels no longer refer to such and such a date before or after Christ—B.C. or A.D., as we say in our pious, medieval fashion; they speak of "Before Our Time Reckoning" or "Our Time Reckoning", so that the fall of the Roman Empire, for instance, occurs for East Berliners in the fifth century of their "time reckoning".

The authorities have not yet got around to devising a wholly new calendar to follow up this change, as did the leaders of the French Revolution, who started their time reckoning with the "Year 1" of the Republic and divided their calendar into 10 new months—*Thermidor*, *Frimaire*, etc. But they have introduced a new set of festivals to replace those of the Christian era—I mean, Our Time Reckoning. In East Berlin, the government encourages parents to give their children a *Jugendweihe* ceremony, a secular dedication to the state when they reach the age of puberty, instead of having them confirmed in church. By the same token, instead of St. Swithin's Day, Whitsun, Shrovetide or Hallowe'en, the calendar is studded with such events as the Day of the Co-Workers of Commerce (third Sunday in February), the Day of the National People's Army (March 1), the Day of the People's Police (July 1), and the Day of Public Health (December 11).

On a visit to East Berlin you will see representative members of the organizations for whom these festivals are named, notably the People's

In an unusual display of abandon during a May Day parade, young East Berliners climb on to a fan-shaped canopy that roofs the entrance to an exhibition hall, one of a pair that stands in the vast Alexanderplatz development. This complex of shops, offices, hotels and flats is East Berlin's trade and tourist showpiece.

Army and the People's Police, for the streets are full of figures in uniform. Perhaps the proportion of uniforms to mufti is not so high as I remember it from Berlin, 1938, but the difference is trifling.

When you get to know the new revolutionary life-style of East Berlin, it turns out to be surprisingly compatible with the late, unlamented military traditions of the old Prussia. Walking around the *Stadt Mitte*, the centre of old Berlin, I often get the uncanny feeling of having been set down in the middle of a Second World War movie. DDR army uniforms look very much like those of the Wehrmacht, and that colonel striding purposefully towards you carrying the inevitable briefcase, with a couple of lieutenants struggling to keep up, could be the ghost of Erich von Stroheim in *La Grande Illusion*. He wears the expression of seriousness and dedication that can be seen on so many East Berlin faces; it seems to be prerequisite to a successful career in the service of the DDR, whether in or out of uniform.

Watching the state functions or party congresses of East Germany on television, what strikes home most forcibly is that everyone in an official position has the same stern-faced look of determination; the political leaders, army officers and higher functionaries never break into a smile. Life, they seem to say, is not a laughing matter. The DDR, as a result, is easily the most earnest country I have ever known; and I often find myself remembering what the playwright Bertolt Brecht once said: "To live in a

A coach halts outside the original gate built by Friedrich Wilhelm I in 1734.

A German cartoon depicts Napoleon stealing the Goddess of Victory.

Tidal Gate of History

The gigantic Brandenburg Gate, completed in 1791 by Carl Gotthard Langhans, replaced one of the 18 modest portals in the wall built around Berlin half-a-century before. Since then the violent tides of German history have washed over it again and again. First despoiled in 1806, when Napoleon temporarily seized its crowning statue, the Goddess of Victory, the gate has been repeatedly battered by war and revolution. It became a government strong-point during the Left-wing uprising of 1919 and a goal of Soviet troops assaulting the city in 1945. Now fully restored, it stands a few yards east of the concrete barrier that divides Berlin.

Triumphant Soviet troops wave their banners over the shattered Victory statue in May, 1945. A replica, cast in West Berlin, was hauled into position in 1959.

Government marksmen, ready to fire at rioters, kneel by the huge wheels of Victory's four-horse chariot—the Quadriga—during the 1919 communist uprising.

During the 1953 revolt against communist rule, East Berliners march beneath the Brandenburg Gate bearing traditional German flags of black, red and gold.

country without a sense of humour is unbearable; but it is even more unbearable in a country where you need a sense of humour." How, I wonder, did Brecht fare when he settled in the East after the war?

When you walk along Unter den Linden, the principal avenue of East Berlin, you will find further evidence that not everything in the capital of the DDR is new or revolutionary. At the Neue Wache, a guardhouse in the shape of an ancient temple, built in 1818 by the great neo-classical architect Karl Friedrich Schinkel and now called the Monument to the Victims of Fascism and Militarism, you can watch a ceremony in the best Prussian tradition: the changing of the guard of honour, in goose-step, every half-hour. Every Wednesday there is also a full dress goose-stepping parade, complete with Prussian military band playing taratara, which would have swelled the heart of Frederick the Great. (It might also suggest there is still some truth in Friedrich Nietzsche's dictum that what it takes to make a good Prussian is obedience and long legs.)

Lest this penchant for goose-stepping seems to contradict what I have said about Berlin being a city without living traditions, lacking a sense of continuity with the past, let me hasten to add that it is: 1) an exception that proves the rule; 2) just a knee-jerk reflex action on the part of those charged with training the People's Army—they had been trained in the Wehrmacht, and that, in turn, had been trained by the Prussian officers of the First World War, thus forming a master-to-pupil chain stretching back to Frederick's famous Grenadiers; 3) a wonderful way of limbering up the muscles, since the leg must be kicked straight out to the height of the kicker's waist, like those of a high-stepping French can-can dancer, but with more precision and no flouncing.

According to the DDR authorities, this display of martial gymnastics is intended, not as a revival of the old German militarism, but as an expression of the "military mastery and iron discipline" required for the current "peace offensive". We can all breathe easier. Moreover, September 12 appears on the East German calendar as the Day of Struggle against Fascism and War, so that all this marching and countermarching can be written off as mere preparatory exercises for the "war against war".

If you can believe that, you should be able to accept the good intentions of other departments of the East German machinery of state. You may even learn to think of the *Stasis* in a new and kindly light. *Stasis* (the word rhymes with the way Winston Churchill used to pronounce Nazis) is East Berlin jargon for members of the DDR's Staatssicherheitsdienst, or State Security Service; but they of course have no relation to the Gestapo (short for Geheime Staatspolizei, or Secret State Police) of not so long ago. No, there is no continuity of traditions in modern East Berlin—unless you consider that continuity, like beauty, lies in the eye of the beholder.

Even without the uniforms, the heart of East Berlin resembles nothing

A disabled spectator at May Day festivities in Alexanderplatz (above) glances through the holiday edition of the "Berliner Zeitung". His conspicuous red tammy suggests that he is more truly individualistic than the young East Germans (right) at Treptow amusement park in their conventional patched denims.

so much as a giant parade ground. Its streets are wide and wind-blown; its vast squares are ideally suited to mass demonstrations (of solidarity, needless to say). Obviously, the architects responsible for the city's post-war reconstruction were schooled in the grand manner of the sweeping vista, and they had a lot of open space to work with: the Second World War had reduced much of the old city centre to rubble.

Clearing up the mess has been a long and tedious process, and the scars of war are still much in evidence. Some of the residential districts just beyond the centre have a dreary, beat-up look as though the war had just ended, their houses pock-marked by bomb fragments and shell splinters. But since rebuilding ranks high on the list of DDR priorities, throughout East Berlin there are construction sites for new buildings and even whole new streets and districts in the making.

In East Berlin are some of the longest, if not the highest, apartment houses in the world, with unbroken façades that may run the length of an entire block and curve to turn the corner, their shoebox austerities relieved only by mosaic murals and other works of airport art. Most new buildings are constructed of prefabricated sections; what the guidebook identifies as *silikatspritzputzveredelte Betonbrüstungsplatten* (concrete slabs sprayed with silicone cement) have helped the designers to economize on labour if not on syllables. The overall effect is grey, impersonal and rather brutal. I think longingly of Paris and its sanctuaries of the soul: the cafés and bistros where you can meet your friends, read a paper, watch the world *en passant*.

One of the problems, I think, is that the major avenues are crowded only on mass-demonstration days. Most of the time there is an emptiness in the streets that gives them a ghostly, even surrealist atmosphere. Life in East Berlin never seems to reach what the physicists call "critical mass". Before the war there were nearly twice as many people living in the same space. Now, with just over a million people, the capital of the DDR suffers much more from under-population than West Berlin. It must have been rather like this in Rome during the Middle Ages, when there were 100,000 people living in the ruins of a city that had once accommodated two million: life in the empty shell of someone else's grandeur. Only at night, among the old buildings around the former Royal Opera House, does the city recapture some of its former magic and elegance. Then the shabbiness disappears, and darkness shrouds the bombed out churches that form the backdrop to the illuminated façades of classical Berlin, the Athens on the River Spree.

The centrepiece of classical Berlin is Unter den Linden (literally "Under the Lime Trees"), the avenue which traditionally formed the east-west axis of the city. For 300 years it was the main political artery of the city, the scene of countless pageants and reviews, the parade ground of Prussian and, later, all-German power. Even now it is East Berlin's most imposing and most famous avenue.

Behind the pale strip of the Wall, East Berlin is dominated by glittering modern blocks that rise from the city's old centre and by the 1,197-foot TV tower, whose

stainless steel pod reflects the harsh sun in a fiery cross. With typical irreverence, Berliners call this striking phenomenon "the Pope's revenge".

At its western end rises the Brandenburg Gate, the most striking symbol of Athens on the Spree. It is a majestic gate resting on 12 splendid Doric columns; its perfect proportions are based on those of the Propylaea of the Acropolis. On top is the Goddess of Victory (or Peace, depending on which period of German history you choose), her chariot drawn by four prancing horses. She and her chariot are known collectively as the Quadriga. Illuminated at night in greenish copper splendour, the Quadriga conjures up visions of an earlier, happier Berlin—the Berlin of the Romantic poets, of Ludwig Tieck and Friedrich Schlegel, of E. T. A. Hoffmann and Heinrich Heine, who used to drive through this ornamental gateway on their way to the greensward in the Tiergarten or the Grunewald. Now nothing can go through here: the Wall dividing East from West passes just a few feet beyond the gate.

The Quadriga was the work of one of the greatest of the German Romantic artists, the sculptor-architect Gottfried Schadow; it commemorated the Peace of Basel between France and Prussia in 1795. When Napoleon captured Berlin in 1806 he had the sculpture hauled down and taken to Paris as war booty. The Quadriga came back again after Napoleon's defeat in 1814, but this time an iron cross and a Prussian eagle were added to the ensemble before it was put over the gate once more. Originally the Quadriga had faced east; the goddess was seen to be bringing peace to the city. Later, in the second half of the century, it was turned round to face the west, with a view to bringing victory to the Prussian legions marching out through the gate on the way to the next war. Then came the First World War: the Armistice, revolution, street-fighting in Berlin. The Brandenburg Gate became an observation post for government troops. Light artillery was set up at ground level and, up above, soldiers with rifles were perched alongside the goddess in her chariot.

During the Second World War both the gate and the sculpture were badly damaged and what was left of the goddess and her horses was taken down. Afterwards the stonework of the gate was meticulously restored by the East Berliners; and in a rare gesture of co-operation, West Berlin contributed a replica of the original sculpture, based on plaster casts that had been kept in storage in the West. But the DDR authorities carefully removed the iron cross and Prussian eagle before hoisting the goddess back to the top of the gate; and true to the spirit of the "peace offensive", they faced the Quadriga eastwards again, bringing peace (as the local tour guides are careful to point out) to Berlin, capital of the DDR.

Many of the other great monuments of Berlin's Athenian epoch on Unter den Linden have also been resurrected from the ruins, although they have mostly undergone changes of personality in the process. The temple-like Royal Opera House built for Frederick the Great in the 1740s, which now serves as the home of the State Opera of the DDR, has changed least of all. Its interior has been restored in the purest rococo style; and

Two posters on a pillar in Alexanderplatz mark the Ninth Congress of the SED, the East German Communist Party. The heroic, 1920s style of the top poster contrasts oddly with the trendy, advertising approach of the one beneath it, but the message is the same: all East Berliners must show solidarity with the Party.

although the building is not large by opera-house standards (it seats only 1,500), it makes up in glitter what it lacks in size. A performance here can be a glamorous occasion, attended by beautiful women from the Third World embassies, high-ranking Soviet and DDR officials, and even by a scattering of French and British officers from the Western sectors who make a habit of going to the opera in the East.

Other ex-royal buildings have been converted to serve new functions. The old Prinzessinnenpalais, once the home of three princesses, is now in a more egalitarian age an eating place capable of serving 500 people in a "wine restaurant", a coffee house and a "nightbar" that are popular with visiting tourists and officials from Eastern bloc countries. On the other side of Unter den Linden, behind the Neue Wache with its goose-stepping guards, stands one of the smaller neo-classical buildings, the Singakademie where Mendelssohn revived Bach's St. Matthew Passion in 1829: it has become the Maxim Gorki Theatre.

Next to it Humboldt University occupies a restored palace originally built for Prince Henry, brother of Frederick the Great. In 1810 the palace was turned over to the newly founded University of Berlin, which following the Second World War, was renamed after its founder Wilhelm von Humboldt, brother of Alexander, the naturalist and explorer. If you have a pass to go inside, you will see a marble bust of one of the best known of the university's former students, Karl Marx, together with a characteristic quotation: "The philosophers have merely interpreted the world in different ways; what really matters, however, is to change it." The adjacent old Royal Library now also belongs to the university. A bronze plaque identifies it as a building of historic importance: "Lenin worked in this building in 1895."

Near the eastern end of Unter den Linden stands the old Zeughaus, or Armoury, where the proud Hohenzollern monarchs displayed their captured cannon and battle-flags. Little boys used to be brought here for their first inspiring whiff of Prussian *Kampfgeist* (fighting spirit). They were even allowed to pat the barrels of the cannon—a very special privilege, since as everyone knows it is forbidden to touch anything in a German museum. The DDR has installed in this 17th-Century building a "Museum of German History" focusing on new kinds of heroes in place of the generals and meat-butchers who were once glorified here: fighters for human rights against Hohenzollern tyranny, fighters for socialist labour against capitalist exploitation, fighters for the brotherhood of man against sectarian nationalism. But no museum of German history, however idealistic, could get along without a certain minimum of war *matériel*: on a recent visit I noticed a boy of about seven, accompanied by his rather nervous grandmother, who was having the time of his life playing among the guns and uniforms of the Napoleonic wars. He was patting the cannon in a friendly and familiar way.

Window Dressing

Although East Berlin's central business district has become communism's neon-lit showcase, with modern shops full of desirable consumer goods, the quiet back streets reveal a different aspect of commerce east of the Wall. The windows of little establishments, some state-owned but many still in the hands of small entrepreneurs, are dressed in sparse, modest style reminiscent of the Great Depression of the 1930s. Even at Christmas, when these photographs were taken, their window displays convey an impression of austerity rather than seasonal abundance.

The goods and services offered by these grey little shops are not often of a nature or quality to excite widespread customer interest. The trade done by most of them is minuscule compared with that enjoyed by big government-operated stores. But these small retailers manage to attract enough customers to stay in business, and, as a group, they continue to make an important contribution to the economy of East Berlin, as well as to its mood and general appearance.

A cardboard cyclist advertises a bicycle shop that does not sell bicycles, scarce items in East Germany; the shop offers customers only spare parts and repairs.

An East German flag is displayed in the window of a state-run betting shop.

This shop takes used bottles and paper for a state-managed recycling scheme.

Several samples of a photographer's work include a client's beloved pet dog.

A vase of fir sprigs shares space with orthopaedic garments and foot supports.

Behind this sombre window the Ministry of Culture sells theatre tickets.

A hairdresser's window makes a modest seasonal departure from drabness.

Not far from the old Zeughaus is the famous "Museum Island" with its cluster of five interlocking Greek temples: a German Acropolis, but without a hill to stand on. Before the war this was one of the world's most impressive museum complexes. Although it was badly battered by bombs, it has long since resumed its former function, and its remaining ruins are scheduled for renovation.

The site at the eastern end of the great avenue, where the modern Palast der Republik now stands, once boasted the royal palace of the Hohenzollerns. The palace dominated the centre of the old city, occupying a large tract of land that the second Hohenzollern monarch, Friedrich "Irontooth", had extorted from the town fathers, and on which he had built a fortress residence in the 1440s. A century later, during the great Renaissance rage for palace-building that swept from Italy across Europe, a sumptuous *palais* was erected on the same spot. Later additions turned it into a baroque palace of 1,200 rooms—a German Versailles which, with its adjoining Lustgarten (pleasure garden), was admired by architectural historians as "the most beautiful example of baroque building in the whole of northern Germany".

During the short-lived revolution at the end of the First World War, the palace became a focal point of armed resistance: from one of its porticos, Karl Liebknecht, leading spokesman of the radical Spartakist movement, proclaimed a German socialist republic. (Shortly afterwards he was murdered while under arrest, together with that formidable woman revolutionary, Rosa Luxemburg, whose body was later found floating in the Landwehr Canal.)

Under the Weimar Republic, the palace was turned into a museum, and in the Second World War it was damaged by fire, but not irreparably. The new government of the Soviet sector, however, was not nostalgically inclined towards the foremost relic of imperial Germany. The building was declared unworthy of reconstruction and its demolition became something of a propaganda exercise. Only Karl Liebknecht's portico was preserved, to be installed in a far more mundane government building. The former Lustgarten, in a significant change of emphasis, became the Marx-Engels Platz, scene of the great May Day parades and mass demonstrations that were one of the specialities of the DDR regime under Walter Ulbricht's leadership.

Whatever the ideological motives, the architectural effect of razing the palace and replacing it with the new Palast der Republik was comparable to tearing down the Louvre to make room for the Montparnasse Tower, the 56-storey skyscraper that now disrupts the skyline of Paris. Except that in this case the conventional modern tower has been laid on its side: the Palast der Republik is only five storeys high but 600 feet wide, an immense shoebox with glass sides. Instead of 1,200 rooms for royal living it contains space for the DDR parliament, or Volkskammer, and an auditorium seating 5,000 people, as well as what a guidebook refers to as "several gastronomic establishments". (That, I may add, goes almost without saying. No self-respecting landmark in Germany, East or West, would be complete without its "gastronomic establishment", or *Gaststätte*, where sightseers and hikers may partake of refreshment after having gazed upon the sight they came to see.)

The Palast der Republik may rate two stars in a gastronomic guide, but it is doubtful whether it will ever win a prize for architectural merit. It stands, pompous and contemporary, in glaring contradiction to the neo-classical survivors down Unter den Linden. The architects of post-war East Berlin may be accomplished engineers, but they seem to have no sense of the continuity of a cityscape.

The oldest buildings in Berlin, the medieval churches, have not fared much better at the hands of the DDR town planners than the palace and Lustgarten. The earliest surviving structure in the inner city, the Nikolaikirche—founded in the 13th Century—has been in ruins ever since the war, and no one knows if it is to be restored. The Klosterkirche, once the most important Gothic building in Berlin, now consists of some crumbling walls open to the sky. Only the centrally placed 13th-Century Marienkirche (St. Mary's Church)—the second-oldest in Berlin—has been restored. It stands, shabby and rather forlorn, on the huge square opposite the red-brick town hall; its spire is completely dwarfed by the giant television tower that rises from the same square to a height of nearly 1,200 feet.

This is a juxtaposition that only an architectural imbecile would have made, comparable to putting the Eiffel Tower just behind Notre-Dame. The East Berlin authorities are very proud of the thing, however, since they regard it as a visible symbol of their undeniable genius for solving the technical problems of building a cloud-scraping tower on the shifting sands of the city's subsoil. Indeed, theirs is second in height only to Moscow's television tower (perhaps only a certain diffidence made them stop where they did). With its seven-storey studio and restaurant pod at 600-odd feet, it looks to me like a cherry on a cocktail stick. Berliners of East and West, who can see its asparagus-tip antenna from miles away, call it *Telespargel* (telly-asparagus). On clear days the sun's rays bounce off the gleaming surface of the stainless steel pod to form a dazzling cross of light—a phenomenon known locally as "the Pope's revenge".

The Marienkirche below the tower is huddled into the ground, as if cringing in embarrassment at these garish new surroundings; since the Middle Ages the level of the square has risen considerably with the addition of new layers of paving. One day, on the steps leading down to the church, I was stopped by an old woman who wanted to chat. Old ladies in East Berlin, I have found, are very pleasant and direct because they have nothing to fear: the *Stasis* take no interest in them, nobody wants anything from them; they can always speak their minds. I happened to be with a young woman who possessed a radiant smile and a nice set of teeth to go with it. The old woman noticed these teeth and took the trouble to point out how lucky my friend was. "You have beautiful teeth," she said, and then, with a radiant smile of her own, showed us her gums, in which not more than seven or eight prominent teeth were left standing.

She told us she was 83 and had come to Berlin as a young country girl from the Lüneburg district in 1917. That was still in the Kaiser's time; ah yes the Kaiser's time—those were the good old days. "I used to have beautiful teeth like yours," she said nostalgically to the young woman. "But now I have hardly any left."

I told her she was beautiful anyway; rarely have I seen a face that communicated so much spontaneous friendliness and goodwill—a real Berlin face. And she had known enough to keep her remaining Kaiser's-time teeth rather than have them replaced with a set of new-fangled dentures which would only have given her a plastic grin. It occurred to me, suddenly, that this lady had been sent to me as a Berlin metaphor: this city, too, can be unexpectedly beautiful in its gap-toothed vistas, where stumps of church towers and walls of past palaces rise at intervals from the bombed empty spaces.

The perceptions of a new visitor to East Berlin inevitably depend on whether he comes to it from the East or the West. Westerners may be struck first by its generally dreary and shabby air, but to tourists from the Soviet-bloc countries, East Berlin is a model city where projects that are still in the planning stage in other communist capitals have already come to pass. "To us, a trip to East Berlin is almost like going to Paris," a visiting Russian intellectual explained to me. "The shops are full of goods like radios and cameras that are not readily available in Moscow, Budapest or Prague. Prices are very favourable. The hotels are extremely comfortable and spacious. Everything—especially the service—functions more efficiently than we're accustomed to. The music here is excellent and the theatres produce many plays that we have never seen in Moscow. For us it's always a gala occasion to come to Berlin—and some day I hope to be allowed to visit West Berlin to see the capitalist side of the city."

A Czechoslovak writer with whom I walked around East Berlin also expressed great admiration for the city's recent achievements in public housing: "Here they have the most efficient building methods of any country in Eastern Europe. In a few more years they will have wiped out the older parts of the city and replaced them with new blocks of apartments and office buildings. Their methods of building with prefabricated sections are gradually being imitated by our own people, although we have a lot of catching up to do. All in all, the East Germans are very efficient, but we Czechs have one or two important reservations: we think they have no

Almost empty, the bleak, snow-swept expanses of Leninplatz in East Berlin stretch beneath the looming bulk of two proletarian monuments: a statue of Lenin in red Ukrainian granite, and a multistorey megalith of collective housing.

sense of scale, and no idea how to have a good time. For all their efficiency they don't know how to enjoy themselves. It's as though after the war they never really learnt to relax and live."

To visitors from the West, East Berlin offers a glimpse of a nation which, according to its leaders, has already passed through the initial phase of socialism and is now on the road to true communism. This, I presume, will mean the nationalization of the last vestiges of private enterprise in the DDR —the small factory that turns out toys and dolls, for example, or the neighbourhood baker who bakes and sells his own bread. The major industries were all appropriated years ago and turned into state enterprises, so that most people you meet ultimately work for the same employer: the government. As a tourist, you eat at "people-owned" restaurants, shop at people-owned supermarkets, fill up at people-owned filling stations, take rides on sightseeing buses run by the government, change money at the state bank and buy government-run newspapers at government-owned kiosks and bookshops.

For many Westerners, this is a wholly novel experience: many thrive on it, others are appalled at the result. "I was intrigued by my first visit to this city where everything has been accomplished by state planning," a young French designer told me. "One of the first things I learned—which we never really consider when we talk about socialism in the West—was that, far from producing a standardized kind of service, you get a tremendous range of reactions on the personal level.

"In the shops, for instance, some of the sales people, knowing they have secure positions, are incredibly rude and pay no attention whatever to a customer's needs. In France they'd lose their jobs in a moment. But in the very same shops you'll find wonderful sales people who will go out of their way to help. I found the same thing in dealing with fellow designers. Some are extremely friendly and warm-hearted—I think mainly the ones who are out of sympathy with the government; adversity makes them very human in their approach to other people. But others—the activists and functionaries—seem to think that a kind of military gruffness and unpleasantness is part of their job. It's a new kind of prejudice that hasn't been defined as yet: not class prejudice, but something like it—a permanent grudge against anyone who does not happen to be a member of the communist inner cadre."

One aspect of East Berlin that strikes Westerners—and annoys the radical idealists among them—is the peculiar lack of equality that prevails in this ostensibly egalitarian system. It is the party faithful of the "new class" who have the best jobs and live in the new apartment buildings. Comfort is hierarchical: the more important the job, the larger the apartment, and the greater the perquisites.

A middle-rank functionary will have a spanking new four-room apartment off the Karl Marx Allee, with a modern kitchen, a television set,

Danish-style furniture, and a picture of Lenin in the living room. He and his wife, who is also bound to have a state job, drive an East-German-produced Wartburg car of which they are inordinately proud, and which they handle with infinite care, ministering to it like doctors when it shows signs, as many do, of developing an illness of the respiratory tract. You hear Wartburgs thus afflicted coughing along all the main avenues of East Berlin, their drivers wearing worried but fatalistic expressions, for mechanics are hard to come by.

To own a Wartburg is something special. But what of those ordinary people who are not party members and live in the shabby, bomb-scarred districts of East Berlin, where the houses have not had a coat of paint since 1938? One of them is a young friend of mine—I will call him Hans—a garage mechanic who considers himself lucky to have a two-room, cold-water flat in a depressingly dingy tenement not far from the Alexanderplatz. It stands within a maze of sunless courtyards and is one of the old 19th-Century "rental barracks" which the 20th-Century idealists swore to tear down if they ever got to power. Housing is in such short supply, however, that the authorities are willing enough to tolerate the old barracks until they can erect high-rise developments to take their place.

Yet, even to obtain his present apartment, Hans (who is a bachelor in his early twenties) had to apply for a marriage licence. An old girl friend obliged, although they had no intention of actually getting married. Armed with this invaluable document, he was able to persuade the housing authorities that he could no longer live with his parents and would need a place in which to begin raising a family. They agreed to let him move into an apartment—Hans himself first had to find a vacancy—and he is now happily ensconced in that rarest of East Berlin luxuries, a bachelor pad. (The girl, his "bride", went off and married someone else, having done her good deed for the year.)

The rent is cheap, but the walls are cracked, a coal stove provides the only heat, the communal toilet is in the hall, and none of the tenants would dream of getting together to brighten up the place with a new coat of paint. There are houses like this in West Berlin—in Kreuzberg, notably—but many of them have tenants' committees that organize rent strikes and demand improvements. Here in the East, however, the lucky ones with apartments of their own prefer to sit it out quietly and not rock the boat. "Enemies of the people" may find themselves without an apartment at all.

When Hans and his friends drink beer at the neighbourhood *Kneipe*, the topics of conversation tend to be limited. Politics is rarely mentioned in public; that is left to the guiding spirits of the Communist Party. The safest, most popular subject is sport. New track records, gold medals, international football victories: these are regarded, at least by the East Berlin newspapers, as proof that the DDR system, with its heavily subsidized

Against a changing East Berlin skyline, a chimney sweep in overalls and traditional top hat drops a weighted rope down an old brick chimney to clear the flue.

A date next to a ladder symbol chalked on a door tells when the sweep will be calling again.

Proud Chimney Sweeps

Chimney sweeping is one of the small-scale industries in East Berlin that have slipped through the net of nationalization. Its guild organization still owes more to 19th-Century patterns of employment than to DDR socialism. A master sweep's business is a small affair, employing two or three journeymen—sweeps who have served a three-year apprenticeship and become fully-fledged guild members—plus perhaps an apprentice or two. All journeymen are entitled to wear the black top hat that is the time-honoured mark of a sweep in Germany, while apprentices are identified by a mere skullcap.

There are 30 or so teams of sweeps left in East Berlin. Each team serves the streets of its own locality, and the journeymen follow a regular monthly circuit through the neighbourhood. Although year by year the proportion of modern buildings with central heating is increasing, East Berlin still contains innumerable houses whose chimneys, furred with the soot of old-fashioned coal-burning stoves, provide an endlessly renewed occupation for the sweeps and their apprentices.

Flashlight, brushes and a rope with round metal weights make up the sweep's equipment. Top hats, very expensive nowadays, have become treasured heirlooms.

and startlingly successful squads of athletes, is superior to capitalism.

Twice a week Hans goes to the cinema—to see East German and Russian films for the most part, but also the occasional French or Italian film, provided its treatment is sufficiently radical to make a point the government wants to have made. Hans likes to visit the great Tierpark (animal park) in the eastern suburbs, which boasts a larger selection of animals than the zoo in West Berlin. And his passion for pop music takes him to the annual "Festival of Political Songs" organized by the "Free German Youth" movement, which brings Left-wing folk groups from all over the world to East Berlin for an annual televised hootenanny. Here, amid thousands of screaming young fans, he can hear "agitprop" music from both East and West: a Canadian folk singer who announces from the stage that he wants to "dedicate this next number to your Ninth Party Congress"; an exiled Chilean vocal group; musical members of the Finnish Communist youth movement; a chorus of folk singers from Kiev. One lyric offers a provocative thought: "Our contradictions are enormous —but they're our own contradictions."

Hans enjoys the music but seems a little dubious about the necessity for so many contradictions. Like most East Berliners, he is subject to terrible temptations and frustrations that would try the patience of a less hardy and long-suffering breed. His relatives in the West can visit him, but he cannot return the courtesy. He sees swarms of diplomats' cars cruise back and forth between the two halves of the city as though the Wall did not exist. He turns on any of the Western TV channels and watches a cornucopia of consumer goods come pouring out across the screen. He is taught to regard the West and its ways with the same pious horror with which the Calvinists once regarded the Popish extravagance of Rome. But it is difficult to work up the proper moral indignation against the consumer society when the DDR government itself opens a chain of "Intershops" where anyone lucky enough to possess West-marks can buy luxury goods that are unavailable for East-marks. And the same issue of *Neues Deutschland* (the official Communist Party daily) that warns the East Berliner against the snares of bourgeois consumer values announces with considerable fanfare that the president of the DDR Academy of Sciences has just urged the nation's scientists "to devote themselves more actively to the production of consumer goods".

Above all, Hans wants to be free to travel where he pleases. He knows that his cousins in the West have been to Majorca, Corfu, the Canaries, even to Thailand. His newspapers show him photographs of DDR development projects in Algeria: he would cheerfully settle for a visit to Algeria, but the best he can hope for is a trip to Hungary or the Black Sea coast of Romania, where he can spend a two-week package holiday.

I know a young East Berlin teacher who would emigrate to Hungary if he could. "Life there is so much friendlier, so easy-going and un-

On their massive Weltzeituhr, or world-time clock, in Alexanderplatz, East Berliners are able to tell the time around the world, from Wellington to Washington, although the farthest west they can travel in their city is to the Berlin Wall, little more than a mile away.

controlled," he says. "The Hungarians don't bother you about everything, and they're not perpetually interfering in other people's lives. I'm sick of never being left to work anything out for myself."

The teacher's frustrations are only aggravated by the enormous Urania Weltzeituhr, or world-time clock, on the Alexanderplatz which he has to pass on his way to work every morning. This monument to DDR internationalism simultaneously tells the time in Australia and the Azores, in Cairo, Tokyo, Caracas and Reykjavik. The only trouble is that East Berlin is a singularly inappropriate setting for this particular device since, in the words of the old joke, "You can't get there from here".

As my friend says, "What's the use of knowing what time it is in Tokyo when I can't go as far as Schöneberg on the U-Bahn to see what time it is on the town-hall clock?"

Like most of the young people I know in the East, both Hans and my teacher friend are convinced that the major political issues have all been decided by the great powers, and they are content to let it go at that. It is in questions of everyday life that they want more leeway—the great ideological controversies over hard rock and blue jeans, for example.

Hard rock is verboten in the DDR because it does not form part of the "cultural legacy" of the nation. It does no good to argue, as I have with a DDR professor of musicology, that this prohibition is wholly at odds with the government's announced policy of encouraging the folk music of the

Torch-bearing Communist Youth gather beneath the floodlit Soviet war memorial in Treptow Park to commemorate the city's liberation by the Russians in 1945.

world's peoples. At any given moment on the East Berlin radio one may hear edifying broadcasts by "folk music ensembles" from Uzbekistan or Timbuctoo. In that case, why discriminate against the folk music of Nashville or Liverpool? The answer is, in essence, that "if it's commercial in the West, we don't want it here".

As for the great blue-jeans controversy, that seems to have been won by the opposition. There was a time when *Niethosen* ("riveted-pants", alias blue jeans) were regarded as dangerously decadent—again, for no very good reason, considering their proletarian origins. I know the son of a Polish diplomat who was thrown out of class when he showed up on his first day in a DDR high school wearing the accursed *Niethosen*.

Still, *Niethosen* and denim jackets have continued to infiltrate East Berlin, where they are the most eagerly sought-after status symbol of the young. People with friends in the West get them as gifts, and those less fortunate pay staggeringly inflated prices for jeans on the black market. One university student I know, evidently obsessed by her passion for this forbidden fruit, paid a West Berlin smuggler more than 400 East-marks— about a month's salary—for a pair of contraband pants. (There are, sad to say, plenty of West Berliners willing to profit from the blockade.)

But wearing of denim is not to be confused with the wearing of the green; it is apparently just a social phenomenon without any true political connotations. Any outward sign of civil disobedience seems to be out of the question in the East Berlin of today. The last manifestation of unrest, the famous outbreak of "*Berliner Unwille*" in 1953, was beaten down with the help of Soviet tanks; and since then the lid has been kept on, very firmly and efficiently, by the *Stasis*. As so often before in German history, a brief outbreak of revolutionary passion was followed by a long period of reaction and repression.

The result is now proudly claimed to be "the dictatorship of the proletariat", but the new life-style of East Berlin might be more accurately described as the golden age, if not the apotheosis, of the Prussian *Beamte* —the same faceless bureaucrat who constituted the backbone of Imperial, Weimar and Nazi Germany. Now he runs not only the post office, the railways and the prisons, but the shops and factories as well.

His badges of office are the leather briefcase, the grey serge suit and an infinite capacity for self-deception. He claims—and may genuinely believe—that he serves a revolutionary cause, an "empire of freedom" no less, in which "democracy may steadily unfold", and which is now "on the road to communism" and the classless society. With these brave slogans on his lips, he helps administer a system of control that, if less noxious than that of the Nazis, is more oppressive and relentless than that of the old German monarchy.

His influence can clearly be detected in all the means of communication. Newspapers, magazines, books; television and radio; posters, banners, slogans, testimonial dinners—all are used in a vast campaign for greater efficiency. Now that the profit motive has been, if not abolished, at least driven underground, the appeal is always to the workers' loyalty and pride: every issue of every newspaper (they all read like house journals) is filled with testimonials about the satisfactions to be derived from fulfilling or exceeding one's production quotas. The ideal citizen of the DDR is that paragon of virtue summed up in the slogan that can be seen everywhere on billboards and posters: "*Aufmerksam, Rücksichtsvoll, Diszipliniert—Ich Bin Dabei!*" (Attentive, Considerate, Disciplined—I Am With It!)

As proof of how well this system works, the authorities point to the bootstrap miracle by which East Germany has risen to tenth place among the industrial nations of the world. I am more inclined to regard the DDR's economic successes as evidence that the German worker, with his sense of duty, can muddle through in almost any circumstances. During the war the most massive bombing raids failed to keep him next day from his workbench—if there was anything left of it. And under "capitalist exploitation" in Federal Germany he out-produces every other worker in Europe.

There is no way for East Berliners to avoid being, as the slogan has it, *dabei* or "with it" at least some of the time. Everybody has to deal with the functionaries of the *Apparat* and make obeisance to the system. Every attempt at private enterprise must have its contact with the state at some point, whether it is a carpenter's workshop, a small bakery or even the humble business of leasing a toilet from a state-run organization. I might have overlooked this neglected aspect of the DDR's economic structure, were it not for the fact that quite a conspicuous number of state-run restaurants in East Berlin have a facility in the basement with a hand-lettered cardboard notice above the door: "This toilet has been leased out." To foreign visitors, this may be a somewhat mystifying message.

In the vernacular, it means: you shouldn't blame the state-run enterprise if anything is amiss, although you may address your complaint to the appropriate higher headquarters. (In fact, the toilets are usually spotless, even if the fixtures tend to be historical.) Also, you must be sure to pay the washroom attendant, an elderly lady or gentleman Cerberus who never sleeps; watching the comings and goings of the clientele with great professional detachment while exacting a small tribute scaled precisely according to the convenience employed . . . (soap and towel extra).

The washroom attendant is, I suppose, another Berlin archetype, perhaps no less symbolic than the Winged Victory on the Siegessäule: the little man who depends on the state for a living. In spite of all the slogans about the dictatorship of the proletariat, East Berlin is in some fascinating and heartbreaking way a throwback to a remote past when the rulers were feared and the workers "knew their place". These workers often seem to belong to the pre-militant era of unorganized labour, when the "working man" was expected to be grateful to his employers, and went about his duties *pflichtbewusst*, as the saying goes, "fully conscious of his duties and obligations"—loyal, respectful, minding his manners.

The workers in East Berlin are still visibly proletarians of the old school. In the West they have been "bourgeois-ized" to the point where you can't tell a bricklayer in his Mercedes from an architect in his Deux Cheveaux, both wearing T-shirts. But in the older, grimier districts of East Berlin I often have the feeling of having been magically transported back to a Berlin, not of Hitler, nor even of the Kaiser, but to the Biedermeier Berlin of the 1840s, when one could tell what people did by the way they dressed.

Here are the brawny beer-truck drivers with their leather aprons, worn to a mirror polish by the rolling of a thousand barrels; the carpenters in their blue midshipman jackets, with two rows of buttons running down the front; the chimney sweeps with their pitch-black suits and tall stovepipe hats, their faces daubed with soot.

My favourite place to watch this romantic parade is Köpenick, the old town that existed even before Berlin was a twinkle in the Brandenburgers' eye. It is a weather-beaten, red-brick district on the Spree, with a small baroque palace standing on an island in the river and a pseudo-Gothic town hall that looks like one of mad King Ludwig's fantasy-castles in Bavaria.

Köpenick was largely untouched by bombs or post-war architects: the gabled houses lean casually against one another; there are factory chimneys on the horizon, small gardens in the narrow side-streets, and cobbled main streets with electric trams that sing musically in their tracks as they turn the corners. Here, at last, is the human dimension so conspicuously lacking in the centre of town: weeping willows at the water's edge, ducks and swans on the river, a scattering of small retail shops, shabby and pleasant. Architecturally, Köpenick has the same simplicity of line that you find in old Dutch villages along the Maas. Something here survives of the original *genius loci*, and it is Köpenick that you should see if you want to understand what Berlin was like before the deluge, when it was still whole, like Paris or Vienna, and not a city with a broken heart.

Echoes of a Prussian Tradition

PHOTOGRAPHS BY THOMAS HÖPKER

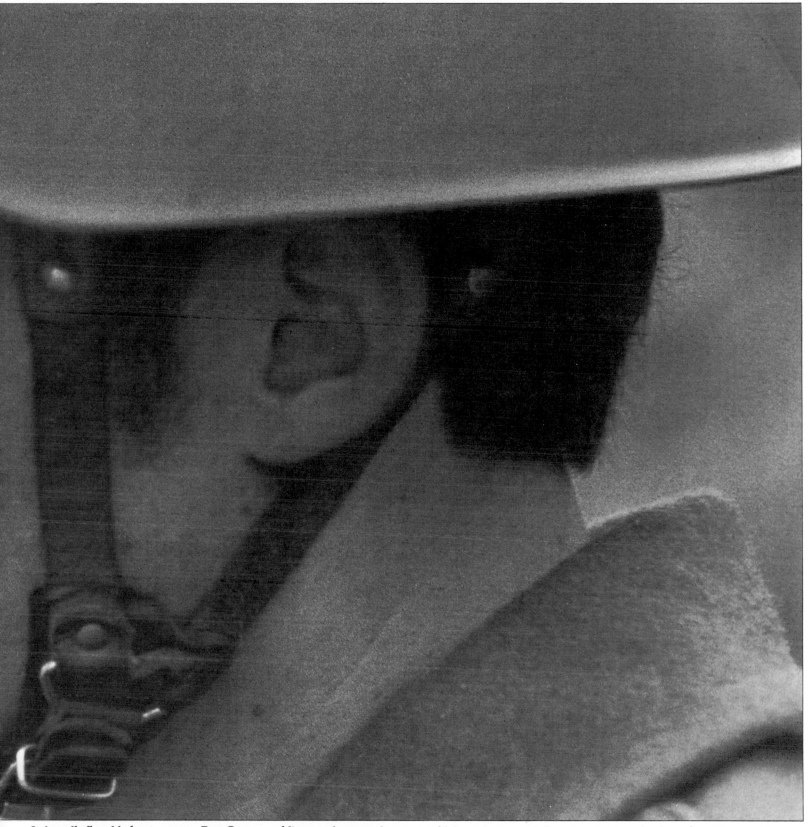

In broadly flared helmet, a young East German soldier stands sentry duty on a cold day, ignoring with Prussian stoicism the drop of moisture on his nose.

In the years just after the Second World War, East Berlin's Soviet overlords suppressed any hint of the old Prussian military tradition. Even when they began re-arming East Germany in the late 1940s they called the soldiers "Police" and gave them Soviet-style uniforms. But the need to engender national pride in the East German armed forces eventually required the camouflage to be dropped and national regalia adopted. Now, members of the *Volksarmee* (People's Army) goose-step down Unter den Linden in military attire closely resembling that of the wartime Wehrmacht. Policemen march about East Berlin in formation and thousands of uniformed factory workers train with weapons in part-time *Kampfgruppen* (Combat Groups). East Germans say the old militarism is dead on their side of the Wall. If so, it has a surprisingly active ghost.

A woman Kampfgruppe member appears as resolute as her male comrade.

A bemedalled Kampfgruppe detachment parades through East Berlin. These militiamen, who train in their spare time, help to create a sense of national esprit.

A passing platoon of People's Police, part of what in local jargon is called "a socialist military collective", infects a woman with its purposeful stride.

A helmeted officer of the East German army music corps relaxes with his Russian counterpart before the start of a ceremony commemorating the Nazi defeat.

East German soldiers goose-stepping down
Unter den Linden turn eyes right in salute to a
neo-classical building erected in 1818.
Known originally as Die Neue Wache, or The
New Guard House, it was dedicated in 1931 as
a memorial to Germans who fell in the First
World War. It is now revered as a Monument to
the Victims of Militarism and Fascism.

6

An Age of Experiments

The whole world has heard about Berlin in the Twenties, the mad, bad era of exuberant sensuality symbolized by Marlene Dietrich in *The Blue Angel.* Those incredible legs, that impertinent Berlin face and that smoky voice singing "*Ich bin von Kopf bis Fuss auf Liebe eingestellt.*" (From head to foot I'm hooked on love.) evoke the essence of an entire epoch. We look back on it now as a golden age because it had that enviable and ineffable thing called style. It produced exciting ideas and fascinating personalities; new images, colours, shapes, sounds and rhythms; the quest for a new consciousness.

It was the heyday of the Berlin film industry, with such classics as *The Cabinet of Dr. Caligari, Dr. Mabuse, Metropolis, The Blue Angel*— and *M,* in which a whole city was shown pursuing a single terror-stricken man in a nightmarish preview of the witch-hunts that were so soon to become an everyday reality under the Nazis. At the theatre there was Illusionism, Expressionism and Social Realism; in the art galleries, Dadaism, Constructivism and yet more Expressionism. Inspired by the visionary ideas of Walter Gropius and his Bauhaus school of design in Weimar, Berlin's architects and designers introduced a new functionalism that tried to reconcile art and technology in buildings, furniture and even advertising typography.

Musically, it was a time of spectacular premières and prodigies; of experimental operas, songs and chamber music; of new works by Busoni, Schönberg, Hindemith and Berg; of concerts conducted by Furtwängler, Klemperer, Kleiber, Walter and Toscanini. Literature produced its own spectrum of genius, with such writers as Alfred Döblin, Gottfried Benn, and the Nobel Prize laureate Thomas Mann and his brother Heinrich.

Even while it was happening, there were many who realized that this was the Periclean age of German arts and letters, and it was taking place right here on the Kurfürstendamm, on Unter den Linden and the Alexanderplatz. Alfred Kerr, one of the city's most demanding drama critics, was not exaggerating when he wrote (more than once): "Berlin is the world capital of the theatre, and of music as well." And the playwright Carl Zuckmayer (who worked as a scriptwriter on *The Blue Angel*) was stating no more than the truth when he recalled that in those days "To conquer Berlin was to conquer the world".

All this, I hasten to point out, occurred before I was born. The sun had already set on this golden age by the time I saw my first play and heard my first concert. I grew up, however, in the afterglow of the

A fashionable gathering watches a cabaret performance at a studio ball in 1925. "Beauty-dancers" who performed naked were a popular entertainment in the uncensored society of Berlin in the Twenties, when the hectic pace of life and the phenomenal level of creative activity transformed the city into one of the most dynamic and talked about capitals of Europe.

epoch; heard stories about it, tapped my feet to its music and met some of its protagonists in later, usually less happy, circumstances. ("But that was in another country, and besides the wench is dead.") In economics there is something called the trickle-down theory, which holds that the wealth poured in at the top stratum will gradually filter down to the *polloi*. I experienced a similar trickle-down effect in the course of my cultural education.

My first awareness of Twenties Berlin was musical and came as something of a revelation. My parents had a hand-crank gramophone and you had to labour mightily to wind it up for four minutes' worth of music reproduced at an abysmal level of fidelity. (You could develop tremendous biceps as a record collector in those days, carrying the heavy albums with their thick records and cranking up the gramophone.) I had begun with the classics: Schubert, whose *Trout* Quintet I must have played a thousand times, Mozart, Beethoven. . . . Then one day—I can still remember my utter surprise and bewilderment—I put on a small single disc with a strange label and heard a heavily German-accented voice sing a honky-tonk ditty in a kind of ersatz English:

Oh, show us the way to the next whisky-bar,
Oh, don't ask why, oh, don't ask why!
For we must find the next whisky-bar,
For if we don't find the next whisky-bar
I tell you, we must die!

It was a catchy tune, but the orchestration sounded tinny and spasmodic even for those days, and the words were quite unlike any we were accustomed to hearing from our English governess:

Oh, moon of Alabama
We now must say goodbye
We've lost our good old mama
And must have whisky
Oh, you know why.

That was my introduction to the music of *Mahagonny*, or to give it its full title, *The Rise and Fall of the City of Mahagonny*, a sardonic modern opera in three short acts written by Bertolt Brecht, with a score by Kurt Weill. Not until many years later did I learn that the "Alabama Song" was written in pidgin English because that was as much as Brecht knew of the language at the time. (He was to become a lot more fluent afterwards, when he went to the United States to live for a few years beneath the moon of California.) Still later, I realized that this was the most "Berlinese" of all operas, as well as a remarkable example of creative prophecy. It foretold precisely the fate that was soon to overtake Berlin—here thinly disguised as the "city of Mahagonny", located in a kind of pseudo-American never-never land.

The clean lines and plain surfaces of this office block in West Berlin might almost belong to the 1970s, yet it was built in 1930-31 to designs by the architect Emil Fahrenkampe. It is a fine example of the functional style pioneered in Berlin during the Twenties, but soon superseded by the grandiose and pompously self-conscious architecture of the Third Reich.

In the final act, Mahagonny goes up in flames, destroyed by nihilists who carry signs with such messages as "Let's disown the other fellow". They sing a song about not needing a typhoon or a hurricane because "whatever damage they can do, we can do ourselves". And the final refrain must have sounded chilling indeed when sung in a Kurfürstendamm theatre with the Stormtroopers already marching outside:

Can't help ourselves, or you or anyone!
Can't help ourselves, or you or anyone!

The haunting songs I heard on that *Mahagonny* recording gave me an early inkling, at any rate, of what is now known as "Weimar culture". (The term is a misnomer since it was not Weimar but Berlin that became the focus of German cultural activity during the years of the Weimar Republic.) Later, there were to be other encounters that gradually filled in my rather sketchy perception of what Berlin cultural life was like when my parents were young.

My impression of this lost paradise was derived mainly from hearsay, or what the folklorists call "oral tradition", for when my parents and I left Berlin in 1938 for England and then the United States, I had stopped reading German books, and there were no histories of it, as yet, in English. Piecing together what I heard, I came to the conclusion that there had been giants on the earth in those days. My piano teacher in New York, Augusta Cottlow, had been both a pupil and friend of Ferruccio Busoni, and I grew up in awe of this formidable Italian-German musician who had been professor of composition at the Berlin Akademie der Künste until his death in 1924. He had been one of the most influential musical theorists of his time as well as the most brilliant pianist since Liszt—a Renaissance man who wrote his own libretti for complex modern operas like *Doktor Faust.* Kurt Weill, who had studied with him, called him "the European spirit of the future". Largely because of Busoni I had thoughts of becoming a composer, too.

When I left New York to become a student at the University of Chicago I met other ex-Berlin luminaries: the ageing Arnold Schönberg, for instance, who gave unforgettable lectures (in a barely audible whisper) as a visiting professor of music, and the architect Mies van der Rohe, then teaching at Illinois Tech. It was only when I returned to New York at the age of 20, however, and found myself working not as a composer but a fledgling music critic on the magazine *Musical America* that I received a kind of post-mortem initiation into Weimar culture.

There was the gentle, diminutive Kurt Weill at the première of *Down In The Valley*, his last musical (he died of a heart attack in mid-career, aged 50); the fatherly Bruno Walter describing his years at the Charlottenburg Opera; Paul Hindemith conducting his neo-medieval "music of the angels"; B. F. Dolbin, once the all-seeing eye of Berlin caricature, who now kept the magazine for which I worked supplied with sketches of the

Manhattan musical scene; Erwin Piscator at the Dramatic Workshop; the photographer Tet Arnold von Borsig; the architect Alphonse Pasquale who also transcribed medieval music—and told me that Paul Klee was accustomed to lecturing at the Bauhaus with his back towards the class.

It was with a mingled tone of pride and sadness that these people reminisced about Berlin. I got the impression that those who had actually lived through the golden age, and who had themselves helped to create it, looked back on it almost as though it were a beautiful legend, like the Garden of Eden before the Fall. Only Hermann Scherchen, who had been one of the leading avant-garde conductors of "Weimar" Berlin, sounded less enchanted by the memory. "The Twenties weren't the golden years you hear so much about these days," he told me. "It's true we did some exciting things, but we were always being accused of poisoning the atmosphere with our new music. And the pay was terrible."

Curiously enough, it was a Frenchman, Edgar Varèse, who taught me to see the period with some kind of historical perspective. Varèse, the composer of *Ionization* and *Poème Electronique*, had spent five crucial years in Berlin before the First World War, when he was in his twenties. He had been a protégé of Busoni and Richard Strauss, had worked on an opera libretto with Hugo von Hofmannsthal, and had conducted the Berlin Symphonischer Chor. One of his close friends had been my father's cousin Paul Cassirer, the Berlin publisher and art dealer who organized the first Expressionist exhibitions, and the first Cézanne and Van Gogh shows in Germany. Remembering his friendship with the Cassirers (there had also been cousin Bruno, who published art books, and cousin Ernst, who wrote about the philosophy of symbolic forms), Varèse spent hours with me, roaming through Greenwich Village and talking excitedly about *vieux Berlin*.

He was 70, and the most remarkable man I've ever known; I was 23, and barely able to follow his literary and philosophical allusions, but in his enthusiasm he didn't seem to notice. Berlin, for Varèse, had been a happy hunting ground of the arts. "People think it all started in the Twenties," he told me. "But the Berlin Renaissance was a process that began 15 years before the First World War. When I got there in 1908 it was already a golden age. It was a coming together of the best brains and the most creative artists in Europe. Not even the war was able to bring it to an end. It took Hitler and the Nazis to do that."

When I revisited Berlin in the 1950s, I tried to locate some of the places that Varèse had talked about so nostalgically—Busoni's apartment in the Augsburgerstrasse, for instance—but there was not much left to see. The great majority of the city's theatres had been gutted or razed; the three opera houses and the Philharmonic were in ruins; not only individual buildings but whole districts had disappeared or changed their

Ambience of the Twenties

"Berlin is a city for artists, for the young, for the creative," wrote an acute observer in 1929, "not for idyllic artists who wish to sit on the bank of a pond, dreaming; but for those to whom a melody can come from the struggles of life." In this montage, assembled in the style of the Dadaists, appear some of the people, buildings and events that helped to give Twenties Berlin its dynamic ambience.

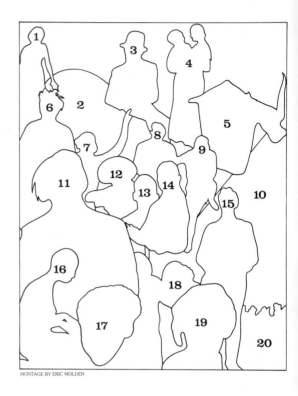

MONTAGE BY ERIC MOLDEN

1. **Beauty dancer at the White Mouse Club**
2. **Rudolf Mosse's publishing house**
3. **Harald Paulsen in "The Threepenny Opera"**
4. **Transvestite hostesses at the Eldorado**
5. **Mary Wigman, modern dance pioneer**
6. **The physicist Albert Einstein in 1920**
7. **Roma Bahn in "The Threepenny Opera"**
8. **Character actor Max Pallenberg**
9. **Pallenberg's wife, actress Fritzi Massary**
10. **Housing for Siemensstadt workers**
11. **Herwarth Walden, art publisher and poet**
12. **Marlene Dietrich in "The Blue Angel"**
13. **Joachim Ringelnatz, poet and painter**
14. **George Grosz, artist, in his studio**
15. **Ernst Toller, writer and revolutionary**
16. **Josephine Baker, U.S. cabaret star**
17. **Brigitte Helm in the film "Metropolis"**
18. **Bertolt Brecht (right) with boxer friend**
19. **Elisabeth Bergner as Miss Julie**
20. **Depositors panic in 1923 inflation**

character. In London neat blue and white plaques mark houses where the famous once resided. In Paris you can find the lantern-lit square where Delacroix used to live and imagine that the painter himself will emerge from his front door at any moment; you can still have supper at the Procope, where Balzac dined with his friends. . . . But for Berlin the best I can do in the way of steering you to such cultural landmarks is to show you the butcher's shop in Charlottenburg where Brecht used to buy his favourite sausages in the 1950s.

Not that this is a really serious deficiency, except for the tourist industry. After all, the cultural history of any city is written not in bricks and mortar but in works of art and schools of thought; in the novels, plays, paintings, operas that it has sent out into the world. Of Berlin's tangible cultural objects, only the more moveable ones have survived—those that could be hidden away in cellars, saltmines or the suitcases of refugees. Thousands of works, unfortunately, were lost during the Third Reich, for it was not so much enemy bombs as the Nazis themselves who destroyed or dispersed the city's great heritage of modern art.

But West Berlin has gone to no end of trouble and expense to reassemble the evidence of its modern Renaissance. There has been a great ingathering of once-exiled paintings and sculptures, with a view to restoring the city's badly tarnished reputation as a fountainhead of art. On the ground floor of the New National Gallery, for example—the beautiful, glass-faced building designed by Mies van der Rohe—there is a chronological procession of canvases that illustrates the beginnings of the Berlin Renaissance in the most vivid and instructive fashion. One moment you are in the late 19th Century: everything is heroic, sentimental, representational. Then suddenly you are in the 20th, and the pictures are harsh, painful, passionate. The latter are the work of the Expressionists, so-called because they looked beyond the shimmering surface of the Impressionists to explore the harsher reality beneath. Paul Cassirer is said to have invented the name: when an art critic, faced with a painting by Max Pechstein early this century, asked Cassirer, aghast, "Is that *Impressionismus?*" his spontaneous reply was, "No, *Expressionismus!*"

I first learned to admire these artists in a set of Cassirer's catalogues that an aunt gave me for my seventh birthday. They showed Max Beckmann's inspired carelessness and the daubings of Erich Heckel; Pechstein's mysteriously distorted faces, Wilhelm Lehmbruck's elongated figures, and the stolid, geometric sculptures of Ernst Barlach. At the turn of the century they had been known as the "ugly painters". "Truly it is not beauty and loveliness that are our strength," Barlach conceded. "Our power lies in the opposite, in ugliness, in demonic passion . . . . " In their painful and deliberate striving for the unvarnished truth, the Expressionists were, to use one of their own highly graphic terms, sounding "*Der geballte Schrei*" (The clenched shriek).

Friezes of conventional nudes share with a banal sex-film poster the front of a seedy cinema in West Berlin's Nollendorfplatz. Now divided up among a bizarre variety of enterprises, including the cinema and an evangelical group, the building was once the home of the radical Proletarian Theatre founded by Erwin Piscator, one of the most innovative of the directors whose work electrified Berlin audiences in the Twenties.

In the days of pre-First World War Berlin, fortunately, there was a remarkably receptive audience that understood and encouraged these attempts to break out of the stiffness and formalism of conventional German art. Nevertheless, a violent struggle erupted between the modernists and the defenders of the status quo. The Kaiser, who regarded himself as the first art critic of the nation, became so incensed by what he saw that in one of his speeches he delivered a diatribe against "Paul Cassirer, who wants to bring us this *Dreckkunst aus Paris* (this filthy art from Paris)". In spite of such eminent opposition (or because of it), it was the Expressionists who managed to carry the day.

Around 1910 Berlin poets, too, embarked on the Expressionist quest for a new intensity of life and language. "My God," reads a 1911 diary entry by the young poet Georg Heym, a leader of the movement, "I shall suffocate if my enthusiasm goes on lying fallow in this banal time. I need powerful emotions to be happy. . . . If only I had been born in the French Revolution, I would have known where to lay down my life." Instead he went skating on the River Havel in the winter of 1912, plunged through the ice and was drowned.

The chances are that Heym would not have had much longer to live in any case. The war that broke out two years later decimated the ranks of the Expressionists: more than a dozen of the best-known poets and painters were killed, many of them fighting for a cause they had grown to detest. But losing the First World War proved to be something of a blessing in disguise for the artists who survived. For the first time the real genius of Germany was given free rein to function and flourish without the constant interference of a pompous and petty government. The republican constitution adopted by the assembly at Weimar guaranteed the citizens of Germany—and hence its artists—far more freedom than they had ever known before. Censorship was abolished; Young Turks moved into the Ministry of Culture; the Berlin municipal government suddenly became interested in modern art. The Twenties, it seemed, were to be a new age of enlightenment and psychological convalescence.

To celebrate the fact that they were alive, many of the younger men were seized by an almost frantic desire to produce a new kind of art—an art, as simple, absurd and accident-ridden as life itself. They called themselves Dadaists: the name Dada, a children's word meaning "hobby-horse", had supposedly been picked at random from a dictionary by a group of Bohemian exiles in Zurich during the war. Some of the young Bohemians descended on Berlin as soon as the shooting stopped. Richard Huelsenbeck, Walter Mehring and Raul Hausmann (who claimed to be a relative of the Baron Haussmann who cut the boulevards through Paris) published Dada manifestos and magazines, gave Dada festivals and held Dada matinées.

In the first of their journals, the Berlin Dadaists mockingly proposed progressive unemployment by the mechanization of all physical labour and the "immediate regulation of sexual intercourse in the Dadaist spirit through a Central Dada Sex Office". Johannes Baader, self-appointed "Oberdada and President of the World", attended the opening session of the official constituent assembly in Weimar by snagging a front-row seat in the Press gallery and dropped on the astonished delegates taunting leaflets that characterized the proceedings as "a manifestation of Dadaism".

George Grosz, a gifted young draughtsman who wanted to become "the German Hogarth", joined the movement to illustrate, among other things, the Dada magazine *Der Blutige Ernst* (*Bloody E(a)rnest*). On one occasion, Grosz paraded through the streets of Berlin wearing a death's head mask and carrying a placard with the slogan, "*Dada über Alles*". As far as the Dadaists were concerned, the Expressionists were now passé because they were too apocalyptic and too well established. "Their easy chair is more important to them than the noise in the streets," Huelsenbeck explained. Dadaism was for activists.

These banknotes for billions of marks, now commonly sold for pfennigs on flea market stalls in West Berlin, are relics of the massive inflation that rocked Germany after the First World War. Although the currency was finally stabilized at the end of 1923, the traditional middle-class ethos gave way to the turbulent, insecure world of pre-Nazi Berlin.

The "Club Dada" inaugurated its short but brilliant life at the Tribune Theatre in Berlin-Charlottenburg with a public recitation by Huelsenbeck, or as he described it, a "sonic litany"—"a painting in sounds of a ride on the electric tram; the yawns of the retired Herr Schulze; the cries of lunatics, and the confusion of everything being at sixes and sevens, while a Balkan express is derailed on the bridge of Nis—and a pig wails in the cellar of the butcher, Herr Nuttke. . . . " There was also a race between a sewing-machine, operated by Grosz, and a typewriter, played by Mehring, with an obbligato dialogue reported to have gone like this:

Grosz: *Schnurre, schnurre—basselurre!*

Mehring: *Tacktacktack*! *Bumsti*! *Ping, ping*!

Grosz (solo on the ocarina): *Tülitetüt*; *Lüttitü*! *O sole mio*! *Old man's river* [sic]; *Mississippi*. . . .

Grosz had been born in Berlin and raised in Pomerania, but had returned to his birthplace because, as he said, "something was happening here". Before long he himself had become the city's most remarkable happening, emerging as the best-loved and most-hated satirist of the Twenties. Although censorship had been lifted, a really rude, uninhibited cartoonist could still get into trouble with the police. In 1920, Grosz's album of drawings, *Gott mit uns* (the motto "God With Us" was embossed on the army's belt buckles) earned him a fine for insulting the armed forces; in 1924 it was a 6,000-mark fine for "attacks on public morality" in the *Ecce Homo* series; in 1928, it was 2,000 marks on a charge of criminal blasphemy with a lithograph based on his backdrop of Christ in gas mask and army boots for a production of *The Good Soldier Schweik*.

For a time, Grosz headed the *Rote Gruppe*, or Red Group, of radical Marxist artists, but soon found himself under fire by the communists as a "petit bourgeois anarchist". As he explained to a friend. "My crime consists of this: that I have also laughed rather maliciously at Left-wing fetishes and party bosses. . . . They have one sacred, unbreakable rule: Thou shalt not laugh at party leaders." In the early Twenties Grosz sometimes dressed as an American cowboy complete with boots and spurs. Later, however, he preferred to dress like a London stockbroker, with a bowler hat and furled umbrella. In this dapper get-up he was to be seen among his fellow Dadaists at the old Romanisches Café, an immense place that was always packed with artists.

The Romanisches Café with its glassed-in terrace *à la* Paris, its revolving door and its seats for a thousand customers was the brain centre of the new, untrammelled Berlin of the poets and journalists, painters, playwrights and publishers. Here you could encounter, deep in conversation, most of the stars of greater or lesser magnitude of the Berlin cultural galaxy. There was Gottfried Benn, the physician-poet who wrote of having sewn a flower into the corpse of a drowned beer-wagon drayman. And Alfred Döblin, the James Joyce of Berlin, whose novel, *Berlin Alexanderplatz*, is the finest ever written about the city. And Walter Benjamin, poet among critics, critic among poets, and the greatest essayist of his time. Here also was the playwright Luigi Pirandello, author of *Six Characters in Search of an Author*, who had come to Berlin in search of a production, which he found.

Other regular customers included the publisher Wieland Herzfelde and his brother, John Heartfield, the world's first artist in photomontage, who had anglicized his name during the war in protest against the prevailing Anglophobia; Max Slevogt, one of the last of the German Impressionist painters; and Paul and Bruno Cassirer. Paul Cassirer disappeared from the clientele in 1924, having shot and killed himself during a quarrel with his wife Tilla Durieux, the most temperamental leading lady on the Berlin stage.

At the Romanisches Café it was also possible to meet the balladeers from the world of the cabaret. They included Ralph Benatzky, who was to become better known as the composer of *The White Horse Inn*; Roda Roda, the journalist-essayist and writer of comic chansons; Alfred Henschke, who wrote elegantly melancholy love songs to nuns; the *diseuse* Margo Lion, thin as a rail and wrapped in clinging black satin, who would appear on the *Wilde Bühne* (Wild Stage) in the cellar of the Theater des Westens to sing, autobiographically, "*Man weiss nicht, ist es der Hungertod/ oder der letzt Schrei der Mo-o-ode. . . .*" (Am I a symbol of famine, or of fashion?).

It was in this frenetic atmosphere that my own mother (then still enjoying her pre-marriage days as a budding Dadaist, although spending most of her time working as an assistant to the bacteriologist Bela Schick)

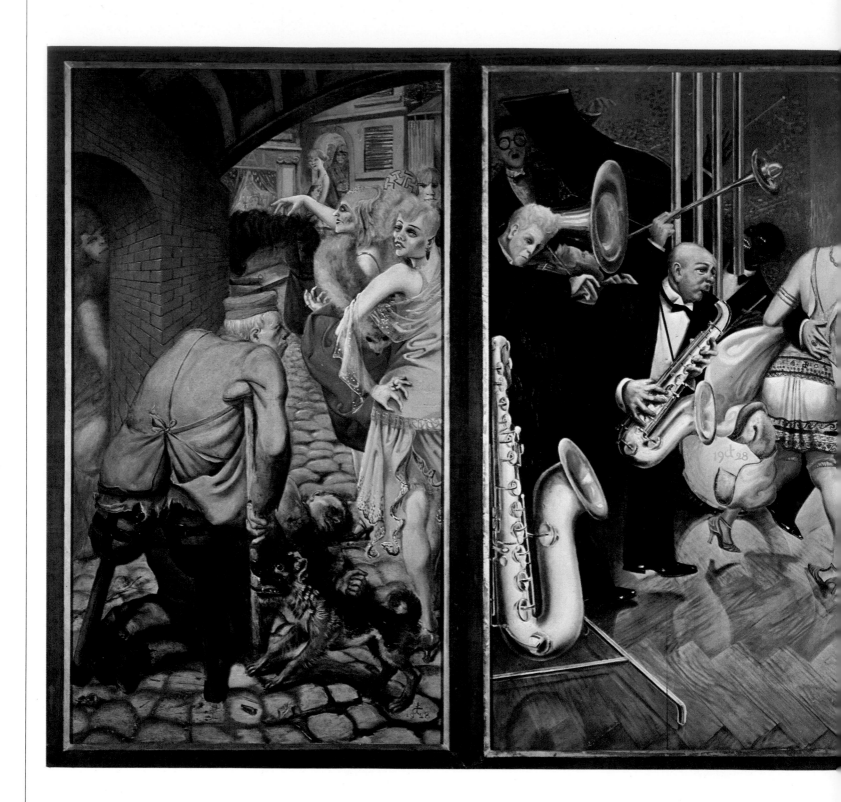

Trenchant Triptych

The paintings of Otto Dix portray Berlin life in the 1920s with savage realism. In this triptych he contrasts the plight of the war-wounded with the posturings of pimps and prostitutes (first panel), and the amusements of the decadent bourgeoisie (second and third panels). The work reflects the so-called New Objectivity, which to Dix meant coming "as close as possible to that which I am observing". He lived in Berlin from 1925 to 1927 and was then appointed professor at the Academy of Fine Arts in Dresden. But the Nazis, who found his work "deeply wounding to the moral feelings of the German people", sacked him and confiscated his pictures. Dix survived Nazism, dying in 1969 aged 78.

Triptych Die Grosstadt (The Metropolis), 1927-28.

achieved a degree of instant, if local, notoriety with a public recital of Kurt Schwitters' poem *Anna Blume*, also known as *Die Blume Anna*:

Oh you beloved of my twenty-seven senses, I am into love
With you—you, yours, thou, thee, I you, you my,
We? . . .

Schwitters' poetry stunned the audience with its grammatical eccentricities. This was only a part of his *Merzkunst*: the art of combining slogans, visual puns, typographical errors and verbal coincidence. Schwitters was both a painter and a poet; a man of limitless talents who wanted to "turn the whole world into a mighty work of art".

In the same spirit of Dadaist innovation, my father, who was then enjoying his own bachelorhood, gave a yo-yo "happening" at the Adlon Hotel, the Berlin equivalent of the Savoy in London. It began with a demonstration by a visiting team of Japanese yo-yo champions and ended with my father doing a "walk-the-dog" with a free-wheeling yo-yo on an extra long string down the banister of the hotel's magnificent marble staircase. Then, impelled by common interests in Dada poetry, yo-yo virtuosity and whatnot, my father and mother decided to join forces. After the wedding— it was 1920—they climbed into a First World War two-seater biplane and flew off to Switzerland on their honeymoon, stopping in open fields along the way in order to refuel. I have a photograph of them as newlyweds, wearing leather flying suits and goggled helmets. Although all this was nine years before I came into the world, I regard myself, nonetheless, as a child of the Dadaist epoch.

In the United States, the "moral decay" of the Roaring Twenties is usually attributed to Prohibition, which enabled the bootleggers and racketeers to get a stranglehold on the windpipe of the nation. In Germany, however, it was the anarchic impact of the 1922-23 inflation that destroyed the old values and transformed Berlin into what the Austrian writer Stefan Zweig called "the Babylon of the World". Zweig was appalled by the consequences.

"Bars, amusement parks, red-light houses sprang up like mushrooms," he wrote. The effect reminded him of a witches' sabbath. "Along the entire Kurfürstendamm powdered and rouged young men sauntered and they were not all professionals; every high school boy wanted to earn some money, and in the dimly lit bars one might see government officials and men of the world of finance tenderly courting drunken sailors without any shame. Even the Rome of Suetonius had never known such orgies as the pervert balls of Berlin, where hundreds of men costumed as women and hundreds of women as men danced under the benevolent eyes of the police. In the collapse of all values a kind of madness gained hold, particularly in the bourgeois circle which until then had been unshakeable in its probity. Young ladies proudly boasted that they were perverted; to be 16

Concrete festoons create an exotic interior for the 3,200-seat Grosses Schauspielhaus, constructed in 1919 by the Expressionist architect Hans Poelzig. Destroyed in the Second World War, the theatre was originally commissioned by actor, director and impresario Max Reinhardt to house the spectacular productions for which he was famous.

and still under suspicion of virginity would have been considered a disgrace in any school in Berlin at that time; every girl wanted to be able to recount her adventures, and the more exotic the better."

No doubt Zweig was exaggerating, but perhaps only slightly; for the desperate economic situation produced a desperate response. George Antheil, the Dadaist composer from Trenton, New Jersey, has written in his memoirs that when he came to Berlin in 1922, "I met a young, prominent German newspaperman and his pretty and intelligent young wife. It was obvious that they were very much in love with each other. It was also rather obvious that they were both starving. It did something very queer to me when, three nights later, I saw this girl in another quarter of Berlin, soliciting. When she saw me she was horrified, turned and ran."

One can follow the progress of the inflation in any reasonably well-stocked German stamp album. Stamps originally worth 75 pfennigs were over-printed, in time, with new 5- and 10-mark denominations; the 10-mark stamps were revalued to 30,000 marks; 75,000-mark stamps soon cost 800,000 marks; then came the stamps of one million and 10 million marks, which were afterwards issued at five billion, 10 billion.

The Berlin mint went on mindlessly churning out more and more paper money and even the printing presses of the Ullstein newspaper head-quarters on the Kochstrasse were requisitioned for the production of this toy-town currency. Large quantities of it are still to be had in the antique shops of Berlin. In the flea market at the Nollendorfplatz you can today buy the inflation money at a mark apiece—bills of 100,000, a million or a billion marks—some beautifully engraved, some hastily printed on only one side. By the time the mad spiral reached its height, one U.S. dollar was worth more than four trillion marks. At F. V. Grünfeld, I'm told, payrolls were shipped in every day in giant laundry baskets. Confidence was eventually restored with the introduction in October, 1923, of a new currency called the *Rentenmark*, and my great-uncle Heinrich, one of the businessmen whose signatures appeared on the new bills, celebrated by papering the ceiling of his office in billion-mark notes.

It was only with the economy back on what seemed to be a firm footing that the golden age of Berlin theatre began in earnest, for even the small, experimental stages needed massive infusions of *Rentenmark* to survive. There were already 30 legitimate theatres in the city; soon there were more than 40, and Berlin became the mecca of theatrical Europe. For six years or so Berlin audiences were confronted with an embarrassment of riches.

There was Max Reinhardt, the Viennese "magician", who specialized in atmosphere and illusion. He had arrived in Berlin in 1894, at the age of 21, to act at the Deutsches Theater—still one of the best in East Berlin and, surprisingly, still more or less as Reinhardt knew it—and in 1905 suc-

Soaring 453 feet above the fairground at Charlottenburg, the steel-lattice structure of the Funkturm was erected in 1926 as a radio transmitter for the Third German Broadcasting Exhibition. Its restaurant, on the platform 180 feet up, quickly became a fashionable venue and is still much frequented by West Berliners because of its splendid views.

ceeded Otto Brahm as head of the company. Later he also took over the smaller Kammerspiele playhouse next door for the production of experimental work. Encouraged by the enormous success of both projects, he indulged his passion for extravagant presentation by acquiring a former Berlin circus site and converting it into a 3,000-seat playhouse called the Grosses Schauspielhaus. To Berliners it became known as the "stalactite cave" on account of the outlandishly shaped sound-reflectors suspended from the ceiling.

Berlin audiences could also experience Leopold Jessner's spectacular recreations of the classics at the former Royal Theatre, which was renamed the Prussian State Theatre in 1918. One of his first productions was a blood-curdling version of Shakespeare's *Richard III*. According to the critic Alfred Kerr, it was a production that "raised the former court theatre to truly royal rank for the first time". Jessner's forte was a stark, abstract Expressionism that focused on words and gestures. His greatest triumph was a production of Frank Wedekind's *Marquis von Keith*. The play was staged against white screens and, with the whole cast dressed entirely in black, the only colour of the evening was provided by Tilla Durieux in an astonishing red wig that reached almost to her waist.

An even greater furore was created by Erwin Piscator with his presentations of "political theatre". The son of a shopkeeper from Hesse, he arrived in Berlin after the war and set up a small repertory troupe that toured the slums and beer halls of the city trying to "revolutionize" the workers through the medium of drama. But the workers had other preoccupations and it was not until Piscator set up a permanent theatre on the Nollendorfplatz in 1927 and began attracting mainly middle-class audiences that his "purposefully shocking" social-protest plays really made an impact. According to his widow, "the bejewelled *nouveaux riches* paid unheard-of fees to ticket agents to acquire their first-night seats", and it was not unknown for these sleekly furbished enthusiasts to spring to their feet at the end of a performance and sing the *Internationale*.

Piscator's innovatory techniques included a revolving stage in the shape of a segmented sphere and treadmills on which an actor could walk without leaving the stage. In his attempts to use the theatre as a vehicle for social reportage, he would get his actors to parade around with signs and placards, and often showed newsreel films to complement what was happening on the stage. On one occasion he even projected the simulated heartbeats of an aviator crossing the Atlantic. But perhaps more significant than all this was the encouragement that Piscator gave to other rare talents. The opening production on the Nollendorfplatz was *Hoppla, Wir Leben* (*Hey, We're Alive*) by the poet-revolutionary Ernst Toller. Later George Grosz provided the memorable designs for Piscator's immensely successful production of *The Good Soldier Schweik*. One hilarious highspot occurred when the doors of a railway freight car opened on a march-past (or rather a roll-past) of dim-witted cut-out conscripts in Groszian caricature.

It was the same rich vein of Berlin satire that gave rise in 1928 to *The Threepenny Opera* at the Theater am Schiffbauerdamm. Brecht and Weill had updated John Gay's 200-year-old *The Beggar's Opera* and transformed the underworld of 18th-Century London into a microcosm of 20th-Century Berlin. They had caught the *Zeitgeist* of the age and articulated it in both words and music. The show ran for 600 performances in Berlin alone and chalked up more than 4,000 performances around the world during a single year—which is something of a record for an opera of any kind. Its revival in more recent times has made *Mack the Knife* an international classic.

Berlin's film-makers, meanwhile, were busy creating a legend of their own on the outskirts of the city. At Tempelhof, where the Knights Templar had once held sway, the brash young director Ernst Lubitsch deftly manoeuvred thousands of extras in expensive costume epics like *Madame Du Barry, Anna Boleyn* and *The Loves of Pharaoh*. He was to be one of the first to make the transition from Berlin to Hollywood without skipping a beat. Later, at Neubabelsberg, on the road to Potsdam, the giant UFA company (which dominated both production and distribution of films in Germany) built what was then the most modern and best equipped film studio in the world. It nurtured dozens of actors, directors and technicians who were destined to emigrate to Hollywood—Pola Negri, Marlene Dietrich, William Dieterle, Michael Curtiz, Peter Lorre. . . .

Many of the leading Berlin directors had an Expressionist flair for images of the macabre: such films as Robert Wiene's *The Cabinet of Dr. Caligari*, Paul Leni's *Waxworks* and Fritz Lang's *Metropolis* had cinema audiences at the edge of their seats. But Berlin produced a new kind of social realism, the so-called "street movies" of F. W. Murnau and G. W. Pabst, in which—anticipating *cinéma verité*—the cameras were allowed to prowl through the streets and alleyways of the merciless modern city.

Berlin also produced a new kind of star. Willy Haas, the Berlin journalist who wrote the scenario for *Die Freudlose Gasse (The Joyless Street)* in 1924, recalls in his memoirs how Pabst invited him out to the studio to watch the shooting: one of the leads was a promising Swedish actress who was hired because she happened to be in Berlin and temporarily out of work. That day in the studio, Haas writes, "was like a dream. She was so indescribably beautiful with her 19 years—yet already she was a great tragic actress. She was a miracle. I stayed in the studio not half an hour, as I had intended, but half a day". Afterwards he could not resist writing her a letter: "Dear Fräulein Garbo. I am the man who wrote the scenario of the film in which you are acting. . . . Had I seen you act before, I would have written a film in which only you appear. I venture to prophesy that you will become the greatest film star in the world."

A poster painted by the stage designer Caspar Neher announces the first production in 1928 of Bertolt Brecht's "The Threepenny Opera", which was adapted from the 18th-Century "Beggar's Opera". Brecht's amoral tale of prostitutes and gangsters, set to Kurt Weill's severe yet winning music, met with instant public acclaim.

Compelled by so much creative energy, composers, writers and artists from all parts of Europe and the United States came to Berlin to see and perhaps also to conquer. "We called her proud, snobbish, *nouveau riche*, uncultured, crude," Carl Zuckmayer wrote of Berlin. "But secretly everyone looked upon her as the goal of his desires. Some saw her as hefty, full-breasted, in lace underwear, others as a mere wisp of a thing, with boyish legs in black silk stocking. The daring saw both aspects, and her very reputation for cruelty made them the more aggressive."

Of course, it might be necessary to live rough for a while, as did the Russian cellist, Gregor Piatigorsky, who spent his nights sleeping on a bench in the Tiergarten. But there was always a chance of emulating the success of the Viennese orphan and former accountant Alban Berg, whose untried opera *Wozzeck* was performed at the State Opera in Berlin in 1925 under the baton of Erich Kleiber, and became an overnight sensation.

The English and Americans came and went in droves: Christopher Isherwood, author of *Goodbye to Berlin* and *Mr. Norris Changes Trains*, gave English lessons and got lifemanship lessons in return; Paul Whiteman and his orchestra received ovations at the Philharmonic; Josephine Baker caused a sensation at the Nelson-Revue on the Ku-damm, dressed in only a bunch of bananas. Not that the serious business of the day was in any way neglected: Einstein and Planck were teaching physics at the Kaiser Wilhelm Institute; Schönberg had succeeded Busoni as head of the master class at the Prussian Academy; Gropius was designing workers' housing for the Siemens electrical engineering company; Erich Mendelsohn built a flamboyantly modern "Einstein Tower" for the Institute of Solar Research in Potsdam.

But even at the height of the golden age, a sinister "counter-renaissance" was already at work. It was made up of people to whom modern art, liberal politics and a cosmopolitan *esprit* were all anathema, and although some of them were merely old-fashioned authoritarians who found it impossible to adjust to a democratic Germany, the majority were something more than that: nihilists, super-patriots, militarists, thugs. They were to form the backbone of the Nazi Party and of its ominously named subsidiary, the Kampfbund für Deutsche Kultur (the Fighting League for German Culture), which declared war on the avant-garde, the Jews, "Culture-Bolsheviks", and by implication, the denizens of the Romanisches Café—everything, in fact, that was not traditionally and identifiably Teutonic (*Völkisch*—"folkish"—was the word they used).

So much has been written about the politics of the Nazis that it is easy to overlook the extent to which they were obsessed with culture, or rather with the destruction of it. Hitler had a paranoid and unremitting hatred for any cultural creation more modern than that of the Wagner era; for experimental theatre, dissonant music, for anything that smacked of the intelligentsia. Far from being merely a minor issue, *Kulturpolitik* was high on the list of Nazi priorities. It was as if they could hardly wait to get their hands on the machinery of government in order to begin annihilating the works of "alien" artists.

In 1930, when the Nazis took over a provincial government for the first time, in Thuringia, they began by destroying Oskar Schlemmer's delicate murals in the former Bauhaus building in Weimar. At about the same time, the Stormtroopers began exercising a kind of veto power over theatrical productions in many parts of Germany. Whenever a work was to be performed that did not suit the Nazis, their strong-arm squads would foment riots in or around the theatre: actors and directors were beaten up, audiences terrorized. Such hooliganism greeted the Leipzig première of *Mahagonny* in 1930, causing the work to be blacklisted everywhere but in Berlin, which tried to remain democratic to the end and was the last to surrender to Hitler's blackmail tactics.

The rest of the tragedy is well known, and there is no need to rehearse it again here, except to recall its calamitous effects on the Berlin Renaissance. Even today many Berliners are unaware of the magnitude of the cultural disaster that befell their city when the Nazis took over. The usual tendency is to assess the cost of the Third Reich in terms of deaths and property ("*Gut und Blut*"). The lives have been counted, and the value of the damages assessed, but the cultural loss to Germany and to Europe was incalculable. What Adolf Hitler and the National Socialist Party aimed at was nothing less than the intellectual stupefaction of Germany, which they achieved in remarkably short order.

Indeed, the real destruction of Berlin began, not with the first British air-raids during the Second World War, but with the burning of the books on March 10, 1933. On that notorious occasion in the city's history, great bonfires were lit on the Opernplatz, next to the State Opera, and students in brown uniforms "marching against the un-German spirit" dumped tons of blacklisted literature into the flames. Dr. Goebbels was on hand to address the crowd and the newsreel cameras: the burning of the books, he said, was designed as a "symbolic action" to show the world that a new Germany "will ascend out of the flames in our own hearts". From that point on it was like a film running backwards. Grosz was already in the United States and Piscator was in the Soviet Union. Now other geniuses who had been drawn to "melting-pot" Berlin began to vanish, one after the other. Thomas and Heinrich Mann, Brecht, Döblin, Klee, Zuckmayer, Gropius, Mies van der Rohe, Mendelsohn, Beckmann, Einstein, Kleiber, Klemperer, Walter, Schönberg, Hindemith, Weill, Mehring, Remarque, Reinhardt, Kortner—the poets and painters, actors, directors, architects, philosophers and musicians, Jews and Christians, Left wing and Right wing—virtually all the people mentioned in the foregoing pages. All those who had made Weimar culture what it was—gone!

The streets were packed with shouting mobs, but the creative people had left the city, if they could, for Vienna (while it was still outside the Nazi orbit), Paris, Prague, London, Amsterdam, Moscow, New York, Mexico. . . . A tragically large number, of course, were caught in the concentration camps and ultimately lost their lives—a process that began as early as 1933, with the detention of men like the writer Erich Mühsam and the Nobel Peace Prize winner, Carl von Ossietzky.

History is replete with tales of rapine and vandalism, of barbarian armies swooping out of the hills in order to sack the city and burn its libraries. But surely the Nazi government offered the first instance, in modern history, of a government in peacetime wilfully looting and destroying the art treasures in its own museums. When Hitler, the former post-card painter, ordered a purge of "Culture-Bolsheviks" throughout the Reich, Berlin was particularly hard-hit. The Kronprinzenpalais was stripped of its magnificent collection of modern paintings and sculptures. Some were sold abroad for much-needed foreign exchange; thousands of others were burned by the "degenerate art" commission, while the Berlin fire department stood by to see that "nothing of value" accidentally also caught fire in the process. In this fashion the Berlin National Gallery lost its German Expressionists and all the rest of its modern paintings as well—by Van Gogh, Modigliani, Gris, Munch, Schwitters, Klee.

It is hardly surprising that this government of book- and picture-burners was doomed from the beginning. As Brecht and Weill had foreseen in the fall of the city of Mahagonny, "We don't need a hurricane, because whatever damage it can do, we can do ourselves." But the other inhabitants, who had to live through this man-made hurricane, had good cause to remember Brecht's bitter and ironic finale:

Can't help ourselves, or you or anyone!
Can't help ourselves, or you or anyone!

7

What Happens Next?

It was a long time before I fully appreciated that the Berlin Wall had two sides to it, as it were. One night as I was returning from the opera in East Berlin and had endured the customary aggravation of going through the DDR exit check at Check Point Charlie, I was stopped on the Western side of the barrier by a green-uniformed official of the West German customs agency, the Zoll. It was a new experience for me; until that evening I had taken my car in and out of East Berlin innumerable times without so much as a flicker of interest on the Western side. Imagine my surprise, then, when the man from the Zoll demanded to see my car's international insurance card, just as if I were crossing the frontier from, say, Holland into Germany.

Since I had left the card at home, I was obliged to park the car in a near-by lot and continue my journey by bus; only when I returned with the papers was I permitted to drive on. Any traveller who is thus arbitrarily deprived of his wheels would probably be miffed; certainly I was. I had always driven out of West Berlin, past the sign that warns "You are leaving the American Sector", with the reassuring belief that what goes out must come back in, and that there would be neither search nor seizure upon my return. It had frequently been impressed on me that the West regarded the city as a single entity under four-power occupation, and had always insisted (although with indifferent success) on free transit between the Soviet and Western sectors. It now occurred to me that, if the Western authorities could impound a car at Check Point Charlie, perhaps they had abandoned this "one-city" concept and were erecting barriers of their own; that perhaps, at last, they had come to accept the DDR view of the Wall as a "state frontier".

Here was a perfect test case, I thought, with which to discover the West's latest views on the status of the Wall, and to put my finger on the political pulse of Berlin. I dashed off a letter to the legal counsellor of the U.S. Mission asking, in effect: well, is it or isn't it a "state frontier"? The answer was not long in coming, and confirmed my impression of Berlin as both the world's most legalistic city and, at the same time, a great, pragmatic metropolis where theory is regularly tempered by practical application: a city whose motto in Latin should read, "*Concinamus descrepantes*" (Let's agree to disagree).

I was assured that, as far as the U.S. Mission is concerned, Berlin remains a single city under the administration of the four-power Allied Control Commission, or Kommandatura. "East Berlin is, to be formal, the Soviet sector of Berlin," the counsellor wrote. "The Soviet departure from the Allied Kommandatura meant only that the effective governmental control of the

The bold insignia on the sleeve of a military policeman declares his nationality and his station at the Wall. "Check Point Charlie"— GI jargon for Checkpoint C—has become part of West Berlin's official nomenclature. It is the only point where non-Germans may walk or drive from one-half of the city to the other.

Kommandatura was restricted to the three Western sectors. Neither that action nor any other, however, has changed the legal status of the Soviet sector or the city as a whole. At the same time, it is an accepted fact that different customs and other financial regulations exist in the Western sectors and the Soviet sector."

This fine balance between theory and practice becomes even finer at the Wall—or, as the counsellor preferred to call it, at the "sector-sector demarcation line". According to him, the customs official I encountered was carrying out normal customs functions which he was authorized to perform. At the same time (that useful phrase again) the checkpoint authorities are frequently urged to be discreet and not to create the impression that the West considers the line a quasi-state border or that it may properly be used to limit free circulation within the city. Significantly, pointed out the counsellor, in spite of the difficulty with my car, I was not myself barred from crossing into the Western sectors. "Like much else in Berlin," he concluded, "there is an effort in the customs field to marry legal and political theory with practical requirements."

Such verbal niceties admirably sum up the outlook of modern Berlin. The one-city concept is still intact, carefully preserved in aspic; but uppermost in most people's minds are the "practical requirements". The years of the Berlin Blockade and the building of the Wall are long past. The survival of West Berlin is no longer the immediate question, and the heat has gone out of the Berlin crisis. The various Berlin agreements negotiated in the early 1970s by the occupying powers have guaranteed unimpeded road traffic between West Berlin and West Germany, and better communications—including direct telephone links—between East and West Berlin. Western occupation rights and the existing ties between West Berlin and Bonn have been reaffirmed. It remains only to work out the final details and settle down to a normal existence, insofar as an existence can ever really be normal in a city divided between two political camps.

The very abatement of Berlin's political tensions has created a new problem for the city. Now that it is no longer in the front line of the struggle between the super powers, it has lost its identity as an international crisis centre. One might suppose that people would have been glad to see the long succession of Berlin crises come to an end at last, but among some well-wishers of West Berlin, at least, the progress towards "normalcy" has caused a good deal of disquiet.

"The whole world looked to Berlin so long as it was being threatened by one crisis after another," a leader of the Christian Democrats in West Germany has said. "The 'open wound' attracted sympathy and *engagement*— subsidies, support, guarantees." Now, the same politician believes, West Berlin will be threatened by the fact that it is uninteresting, lacking in *raison d'être*, without any more dramatic function to fulfil than carrying on its

In the painting: **Für ein vereintes, unabhängiges, sozialistisches Deutschland!**

A large painting, erected in the street by supporters of one of West Berlin's small Marxist factions, represents workers from both sides of the Wall uniting to drive out capitalist exploiters and American tanks—as well as Soviet soldiers (far right). Exhibited in a demonstration to mark the 15th anniversary of the Wall's construction, the painting calls for a "united, independent, socialist Germany".

mundane business affairs from day to day. "Will that suffice to give it life if its geography remains as abnormal as it is at present?"

Many West Germans (they could be labelled the pessimistic school) are concerned that the inconvenience of life in West Berlin—the extra paper work, the special rubber stamps, the long queues at the crossing points, the higher expense of going on holiday—compared with the easier life in the rest of West Germany will ultimately demoralize and depopulate the democratic half of the city. On the other hand East Berlin looks as though it will be made into a show-case for German communist achievements. West Berlin, without any similar political input, will by contrast become less and less impressive. "Not politics but amusement will dominate the scene," one source predicts. "There will be fewer inhabitants and perhaps more visitors. . . ."

The prediction of a decline in the population of West Berlin is backed up by the West German Institute for Economic Research, which has forecast a continuing migration of young people to West Germany and calculates that this, combined with the natural levelling off in the high proportion of elderly people in West Berlin, will cause the city's population of around two million to drop steadily to 1.73 million by 1990.

In my opinion, such pessimism about the future is unwarranted. Even if the population does decline, it does not follow that West Berlin will subside into lifeless insignificance. The pessimists not only pay scant regard to the renowned capacity of Berliners to adapt to circumstances, they also ignore or dismiss as "amusements" some of Berlin's most vital energies, which are strongest in the Western half of the city. As I was told by a West Berlin newspaperman one day at the Press Club on the Ku-damm: "Berlin is a political place, but it is also a lot of other things. We have hidden strengths that rarely make the headlines. Basically, there are four Berlins. Foremost, of course, is political Berlin. But there is also commercial-industrial Berlin, cultural Berlin and, if you like, sexual Berlin. In each of these categories we are unique. We are a four-power city in more ways than one."

It strikes me that the "four Berlins" are the best guarantee that the city will have a worthwhile role to play in the future, even though it no longer functions as a front-line battleground. The "four Berlins" give the city an identity, a personality that will carry it through the less dramatic times ahead. Indeed the Berlin personality has been quietly alive, behind the noise and glare of super-power politics, all along. For more than 30 years Berlin has been functioning as the crypto-capital of Germany, and it is likely to continue doing so. The nation may be divided and the capital may be divided, but—from both East and West—Germans still look to Berlin for a sense of the cosmopolitan, for the bustle of a great metropolis.

The most basic of the "four Berlins" is involved with industry and commerce. Berlin remains the greatest industrial city in Germany as a whole, in spite of its division. West Berlin has higher productivity and in many fields higher wages than the rest of West Germany; East Berlin has a noticeably higher standard of living than the rest of East Germany. One could try to describe this strength statistically: West Berlin, for example, employs just over 200,000 people in manufacturing jobs, mainly in electrical and mechanical engineering and chemicals. Not being an economist, however, I tend to see industrial Berlin in terms of specific people in specific factories. I think, for example, of the skilled craftsman I saw in Spandau in outer West Berlin, producing high-voltage insulators on an immaculately ordered workbench. He represents the best in German industrial achievements. He wears a lab coat that makes him look like a resident physician at a hospital and there is a surgical precision to his movements that might be described as "typically German", except that the name of the man is Ahmed and he is a Turkish *Gastarbeiter*. For thousands like him, industrial Berlin is the pot of D-marks at the end of the rainbow.

Money is not the only benefit Ahmed receives in Berlin. At the company workers' club he can spend his leisure time in the photo lab or at language classes. He and his fellow club members can play tennis, build boats, send their children to a day nursery, borrow books or works of art from a lavishly stocked library and art gallery, and even produce their own television programmes in an experimental closed-circuit studio. A far cry, all this, from the soot-stained Berlin proletariat depicted in the cartoons of Heinrich Zille at the turn of the century. Today industrial Berlin at its best represents an emerging ideal: the proletarian as Renaissance man, enjoying an emancipation and a new fulfilment of his personal talents.

Berlin has long been important as an industrial centre and it has now discovered a special role to play in commerce. With the improvement of relations between the two Germanies, Berlin provides an ideal meeting point for emissaries from East and West. A businessman from Hamburg, in the West, for example, can meet a factory manager from Leipzig, in the East, without either man having to stray from his accustomed political sphere. The emissary from the capitalist world stays perhaps at the Bristol Hotel Kempinsky in West Berlin; the manager of a "people-owned" industry has a room at the Berolina Hotel in East Berlin. They meet for the day in East Berlin, looking at a display of machinery for export, conferring with engineers and drawing up contracts. In the evening they may dine together at the Bucharest Restaurant in Karl Marx Allee; perhaps both will bring their wives, although the conversation may be rather uneasy since each side will try to refrain from saying anything that would embarrass the other. After dinner they may go dancing to the oom-pah-pah band in the fashionable Moskva Tanzbar night-club just along the street; then back to bed in their respective hotels. (The only thing that cannot happen, except in the rarest instance, is that the Leipzig factory manager spends the evening among the bright lights of West Berlin.)

A young painter in the Künstlerhaus Bethanien, an artists' community centre in West Berlin, puts the finishing touches to one of the components for his cut-out facsimile of Adolf Hitler. He is typical of hundreds of artists who find the city a stimulating place in which to work. They live here in greater numbers than in any other West German city.

A world apart from industrial-commercial Berlin is cultural Berlin, the Berlin I know best. Culturally, Berlin is as indispensable to both Germanies as New York is to the United States. It has its theatrical and musical traditions to uphold; its literary *colloquia*, both formal at the academies and informal across the *Kneipe* tables; its historians in the archives, curators in the vaults, librarians in the stacks; its painters drawing inspiration from the crowded streets of Kreuzberg or the sweaty dance halls of the Kurfürstendamm. Its most exuberant form, one need hardly point out, is found on the Western side of the Wall.

As a group, Berlin's actors, directors, writers and academics like to think of themselves as inheritors of the great intellectual tradition of dissent that marked the golden age of Berlin culture in the Twenties. They tend, therefore, to declaim a good deal and take every opportunity to knock the bourgeoisie. A highlight of the West Berlin theatre in recent memory was a revival of Gorky's play *Summer Folk*, at the climax of which the heroine, a good, long-suffering woman of revolutionary ideals, pounds on the table, her face distorted by righteous anger, and shouts at her no-good, lay-about middle-class friends: "*Ihr seid Schweine! Schweine!*" (You are Pigs! Pigs!)

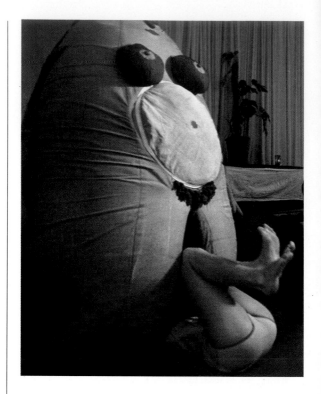

This was considered a great cathartic moment for the West Berlin intelligentsia, nearly every member of which dreams of being able to shake his or her own fist in the face of the exploiting class enemy, and call him *Schweine! Schweine!* The fact that they themselves belong to the affluent, upper-income bracket has little or no bearing on the case: in West Berlin the main thing is to have the requisite amount of social *ressentiment* to make a dynamic impression on your audience. Any play that wants to be successful in West Berlin should deliver a well-aimed kick at the capitalist groin, and it will have the art-loving businessmen and their wives cheering in the aisles.

Of course, cultural Berlin has a less histrionic side that is epitomized, for me, by the secondhand bookshop of Kurt Wegner, last of the great Berlin booksellers. In the years before the Nazi book burnings of 1933, Herr Wegner had his shop in the eastern part of the city. In the Nazi years he was imprisoned for being a communist, and in the post-war years expropriated for being a capitalist. When I last visited him, Wegner was working out of an 1890s apartment on the Schöneberger Ufer in West Berlin, just across the canal from the New National Gallery. His rooms were crammed to the ceiling with literary treasure and he was keeping West Berlin's *literati* supplied with rare books.

Herr Wegner had known all the city's great writers personally since the Twenties, when the Expressionist poets used to dump over-runs of their limited editions on his bargain tables. An hour at Wegner's was better than a course in modern German literature at the Free University, and twice as amusing. While listening to him reminisce about his dealings with Brecht, Else Lasker-Schüler, Ernst Toller, George Grosz, Alfred

Their expressions ranging from enthralled to dubious, an audience of young West Berliners (above) watch a big dummy—schematically female—give birth to a gangling "baby" (left) in a performance by a theatre group called Rote Grütze (Pink Blancmange). Designed to teach children the elements of reproduction, the entertainment typifies West Berlin's matter-of-fact attitude towards sex.

Döblin and the rest of the Weimar constellation, you could browse through shelves packed with fabulous old magazines (*Die Aktion*, for example, or *Simplicissimus*, *Jugend* and *Das Plakat*), first editions of Dadaist poetry, erotic folklore from the *Anthropophyteia*, early works by Albert Einstein— the magnificent detritus of Berlin's most glorious moments. There are secondhand bookshops elsewhere in Germany, of course, but I can think of none other so well-stocked with the raw materials of literary and cultural history from the heyday of the Expressionists and Dadaists.

Just around the corner, as it were, from cultural Berlin—and mainly West of the Wall—lives sexual Berlin. It is not the least of the attractions that bring visitors here from other, more conventional German cities: the call of the wild, if you will. "I've never seen anything like this," a well-placed businessman from Frankfurt told me one day, his eyes still agape with the recollection of the night before. "You can have anything in Berlin—simply anything at all!" He meant, I suppose, that Berlin was a haven, like Lawrence Durrell's Alexandria, for the sexually frustrated from less favoured regions.

Sexual Berlin, like cultural Berlin, prides itself on a tradition that reaches back to the roaring Twenties, when other cities now in the sexual front line —Amsterdam or Copenhagen, for example—were still models of puritanism. Moreover, far from being an underground phenomenon, sexual Berlin carries on as openly and as legally as cultural Berlin, without a false sense of shame. Its attractions are advertised unabashedly in the newspapers, on posters and on leaflets that are tucked under your windscreen wiper if you park on or near the Ku-damm at night. The "Villa Leonardo da Vinci", for example, promises you the "selfless devotion of our young masseuses and

Assuming an air of nonchalance, three university students relax in their off-campus living room, which is decorated with a conscious simplicity that recalls the style of the Twenties. Like many of their peers, they live together in an intimacy that excites little comment in uncensorious West Berlin.

hostesses" at its sauna establishments, which also offer continuous blue film showings, a "bath service", and overnight facilities if desired, either in the centre of town or out in a luxurious villa in the Grunewald.

Berlin is an unusually happy place for dalliances. It's not a matter of what you can get here—most cities in the Western world are fairly grown up by now—but of the spirit in which it is offered. Paris has more sophisticated strip clubs, for instance, but there are laws against prostitution which are still sporadically enforced, giving the whole sex scene a furtive and rather criminal atmosphere. That creates a good deal of uptightness and hypocrisy. In London there are smutty massage parlours in Soho—it's hard to find a bit of style or exuberance. New York has dropped a great deal of its erstwhile prudery, but for a variety of reasons (one of them being that people are afraid to go out on the streets at night) it's still a long way from being a wide-open city. In Amsterdam you can see the girls sitting in shop windows, and Hamburg has a municipally owned sexual supermarket; but the atmosphere in those cities is so businesslike that you might as well be attending a hardware convention.

Berlin, with its history of being sexually unbuttoned, is refreshingly different. There are no laws against doing as you please with your own body; only against exploiting someone else's. Champagne in the bathtub at four in the morning, with everyone laughing and giggling—that's my image of nightlife in Berlin. You have topless and bottomless and indeed reckless and shameless bars and night clubs; yes, a shameless city, if you like. But without hangups; service with a smile. In the summertime, when a couple of totally naked girls show up at a *Kneipe* to have a beer, nobody rushes out to call the police, but nobody looks away either.

Another unusual feature of Berlin is the traditional *specialité de la maison*: the transvestites. They have clubs and bars of their own which resound all night with laughter and the popping of champagne corks. Men dressed as women have been a feature of Berlin nightlife longer than anyone cares to remember: perhaps they are the ultimate revolt against the constraints of the old German educational system, with its compulsive emphasis on order, neatness and obedience. After all, what could be more profoundly disorderly and disobedient than the stalwart Hans's transformation into a giggling, flirtatious *femme fatale* in a spangled bra and dangling ear-rings?

Berlin's transvestites are delighted to perform not only for one another but for the public at large. I shall never forget the expression of pained surprise on the face of an American visitor—a thickset, free-spending gentleman from the Mid-West—who suddenly discovered that the gorgeous dancer who had been shaking her magnificent bare breasts at him from the stage of the New Eden nightclub was really a boy (revamped by hormone treatments and silicone injections). And although I have not made a statistical survey, I am under the distinct impression that at least half the performers on the "Berlin-by-night" circuit are changelings of one kind or the

Transvestite cabaret stars celebrate in their dressing room at the end of a successful show. Berlin, an earthy city whose audiences are discerning as well as sympathetic, has been famous since the 1920s for its transvestite clubs, which combine satire with frivolity.

other—a circumstance that adds a strangely surrealistic touch to the sexual acrobatics that are on display in this pleasure island of limitless erotica.

There is nothing that cannot be found in sexual Berlin, the least inhibited and most satisfaction-orientated city in Europe. "Sodom and Gomorrah!" cry the German moralists. "The new millennium for consenting adults!" the hedonists reply. In either event, it adds to the lustre of Berlin that here, in the heart of tired old Europe, there is so much young orgone energy pulsating through the dance halls, nightclubs and massage villas. Even if it could not survive as an Athens, Berlin would always be able to get by as a "Bangkok on the River Spree".

Needless to say, the idea of West Berlin as a kind of pleasure island is firmly rejected by the city fathers: it does not square with their vision of the city as an "outpost of freedom". But the idea has a disconcerting habit of popping up in different guises. It's not only the city's sexual extravaganza that is to blame, but also the quirkiness of the political landscape; as always in Berlin, one returns in the end to politics. Critics on the Left have spoken of West Berlin rather disparagingly as "the Disneyland of contemporary German history", where tourists can go sightseeing among the mementoes of the Second World War, dream of the golden Twenties, and gaze at the Wall under neon lights. Personally I see nothing reprehensible in that: if Berlin goes on providing visitors with food for thought—even if it's only through a window at the Hilton—so much the better.

In my view the city's function as a place for political comparison shopping will remain one of its principal attractions so long as the East German version of Soviet communism does not undergo a far more radical transformation than now seems possible. I think of East Berlin, in this context, as a "Disneyland": the place where upon payment of a small fee (the price of a bus or U-Bahn ticket) you can enter an alien environment—virtually a different period in history—and wander through the streets of a city that embodies another way of thinking about the world. The nub of the original Disneyland is a fairytale sense of adventure that can transport you to different places and even to different epochs; in East Berlin it is the siege mentality of the DDR government that has placed its characteristic stamp on all the sights and exhibits.

There will be some visitors for whom there is enormous appeal in all this: the law and order, the sense that everything is directed from above by a superior *Apparat* which knows what is best for everyone. There will be others—I dare say the majority—in whom the notion of a whole country that is disciplined and in step will induce a severe emetic reaction. That there is a chance to see this political model for oneself, side by side with the Western alternative, is thoroughly salubrious. Perhaps, in some not too distant future, the world will possess a series of divided cities—known generically as "Berlins"—where international competition will no longer

A boy in an East Berlin playground completes a chalk drawing of a spacecraft which he has labelled USSR in line with the DDR's emphasis on Soviet technological achievements. But in dress, in the length of his hair and in his unmitigated enthusiasm for space flight, he could be a boy anywhere in the West.

involve compulsion and violence but merely the free choice between rival systems. The "voter" would be free to join the system which seemed to offer the more attractive alternative. (Indeed, even now a West German who wants to join the DDR system is free to do so: only in the other direction is traffic prohibited.) It is in this sense that my journalist friend from the Press Club on the Ku-damm regards Berlin as the (imperfect) model for the Utopias of the 21st Century.

Until the happy day when the traffic can move both ways, the essential difference between East and West Berlin will remain embodied in that ugliest and most demeaning of modern political symbols: the Wall. A fearsome and eloquent thing, it continues to goad the people trapped behind it into incredibly daring or despairing attempts to escape. Ordinarily, East Berliners avoid going anywhere near it, for the streets in the vicinity are thick with police and border guards. Security has grown increasingly tight with the years and the odds against escaping have become very short. Even so, ingenious people still manage to find ways of getting out.

The methods currently in use are, of course, closely guarded secrets: once they become known to the DDR police they cease to be of any value to other would-be defectors. But the methods successfully used in the past are impressive testimonials to the inventiveness and endurance of the East Berliners. There was, for example, the S-Bahn driver who packed his entire family and a group of friends aboard his train, and took them down an abandoned spur of track into West Berlin. After his escape, the rails were torn up to prevent a recurrence.

There was a young girl who was strapped beneath the chassis of her West German fiancé's car and driven out through the checkpoint at Heinrich Heine Strasse, her face only inches away from the exhaust pipe. And a young man from the West, in love with a girl from the East, contrived to get her out by hiding both the girl and her mother on the floor of his open sports car. The car was just low enough so that, with its windscreen lowered, it could pass through the three-foot gap beneath the pole barriers used to control traffic at the checkpoints. He went roaring through the checkpoint, squeezing under the barriers with only millimetres to spare, and the border guards were too surprised to shoot. The barriers are now reinforced with perpendicular steel beams, and the slalom course of cement obstacles through which cars have to pass is more tortuous than ever before.

Indeed, the checkpoints have become so cluttered with obstructions that the guards themselves have trouble seeing what is going on. One very daring (and athletic) young man took advantage of this circumstance by running through a checkpoint on foot, at positively Olympic speed. Again, no one was prepared for his extraordinarily foolhardy manoeuvre, and the guards were too stunned to draw their pistols. When he reached the Western side—according to an American military policeman who witnessed the scene—he came to a stop in front of the Allied control post, turned around to face the DDR guards still only 20 yards away, and raised his hands above his head as if celebrating a goal scored in a football match.

For a time during the 1960s organized teams of "flight-helpers" in the West devised ways of getting people out of East Berlin. At first their motives were purely altruistic, and some of their adventures read like a modern-day version of *The Scarlet Pimpernel*. One flight-helper drove a giant steam shovel to the Western side of the Wall, swung its arm over and scooped up some of his friends who were waiting on the other side. Other helpers dug a tunnel under the Wall that enabled dozens of East Berliners to crawl to freedom before it was discovered by the East German police.

Before long, however, the helpers' ranks were infiltrated by gangs of underworld characters, many of whom victimized friends and relatives of would-be defectors. They collected so-called freedom money in advance, made half-hearted attempts to help their clients escape and pocketed their fees even when their clients were arrested and sent to prison. Rival gangs denounced one another's agents in the East to the DDR police, and men were found mysteriously murdered. The ensuing scandals forced the West Berlin police to crack down on professional as well as amateur flight-helpers and as a consequence the whole idea has fallen out of favour. Fortunately, the gradual improvement of conditions in the East have made escape a less pressing necessity than it was in the dark days just after the Wall went up.

Nevertheless East Berlin will remain a great object lesson, even if it becomes more beautiful and acquires more glitter and prestige than it enjoys at the moment. The object lesson of what? That without freedom, nothing can prosper; that order and discipline, however well intentioned, are not adequate substitutes for personal liberty; that the ideal for which so many people have given their lives is not an idle bourgeois luxury but an essential component of human existence.

This is a vital lesson so easily overlooked by those who have enjoyed freedom all their lives. The absence of freedom cannot really be imagined until one has experienced it at close range. No one who visits the Disneyland of Unfreedom can fail to be profoundly affected by the incredible, almost schizophrenic gap between ideals and practices, between promise and performance, in a city where one is not allowed to speak one's mind.

The necessity of freedom sounds almost banal, but it was brought home to me with singular poignancy one day when I photographed two men labouring in a garden on the southern edge of East Berlin. They saw me taking the picture and could tell from my clothes that I was a foreigner.

"Kommen wir in die Freiheit?" one of them asked, pausing for a moment from his work. "Does this mean we [our pictures] will come out in freedom?" It was a question I shall not easily forget.

Berliners All

With earnest hedonism, West Berliners sunbathe in a city park where nudity is explicitly allowed, keeping alive a craze that began between the two world wars.

Berlin has been divided since 1945—but before that it was intact for more than seven centuries. In spite of today's dramatic contrasts between East and West, there are still innumerable citizens on both sides of the Wall who are, above all, Berliners. They are the inheritors of a temperament that took 700 years to evolve—tough, sharp-tongued, stoical, yet sentimental and convivial, too. Different aspects of that personality may be clearer on different sides of the Wall—a certain hectic licence in the West, a dogged puritanism in the East. But no simple polarization could match the contradictions of the true Berliner's nature: there are hints of gaiety and romance in the stoicism of the East, of stoicism in the gaiety of the West. And East or West, every Berliner feels pain because his city is no longer the living whole it once was.

Two young West Berliners exchange glances in one of Berlin's most durable settings — a Kurfürstendamm café.

At a May Day parade in the Alexanderplatz, two members of the People's Police of East Berlin prove that sober uniforms cannot always conceal tender hearts.

A sunny afternoon in a suburban beer garden brings out a capacity for tranquil enjoyment in some elderly East Berliners. Succumbing to the strains of a waltz, two firmly hatted ladies calmly take the floor together, their gestures artlessly recalling the style of another era.

Displaying an impassive—even obstinate—side of their nature, a West Berlin couple refuse to allow rain to hurry a leisurely promenade in the Grunewald.

Big cones of presents sweeten the first schoolday for little East Berliners.

Unable to conceal their emotion, two brothers from a family physically parted by the Wall greet each other after long and unwilling separation. Scenes such as this constantly remind Berliners—and the world—that the political division imposed on their city is essentially an artificial one.

Bibliography

Baedeker, *Berlin.* Karl Baedeker, Freiburg, 1971.
Balfour, Michael, *The Kaiser and His Times.* Pelican Books, London, 1975.
Childs, David, *East Germany.* Ernest Benn, London, 1969.
Delmer, Sefton, *Weimar Germany.* Macdonald, London, 1972.
Döblin, Albert, *Berlin Alexanderplatz.* Berlin, 1929.
Eckardt, Wolf von, and Gilman, Sander L., *Bertolt Brecht's Berlin.* Anchor Press/ Doubleday, New York, 1975.
Esslin, Martin, *Brecht: A Choice of Evils.* Eyre & Spottiswoode, London, 1959.
Fodor, *Germany.* Hodder & Stoughton, 1972.
Friedrich, Otto, *Before the Deluge.* Michael Joseph, London, 1974.

Gallante, Pierre, *The Berlin Wall.* Arthur Barker, London, 1965.
Gay, Peter, *Weimar Culture.* Penguin Books, London, 1974.
Grunfeld, F. V., *The Hitler File.* Weidenfeld & Nicolson, London, 1974.
Holmes, Judith, *Olympiad 1936.* Ballantine, New York, 1971.
Isherwood, Christopher, *Goodbye to Berlin.* Penguin Books, London, 1975.
Kiaulehn, Walther, *Berlin: Schicksal einer Weltstadt.* Munich, 1958.
Kracauer, Siegfried, *From Caligari to Hitler.* Princeton, 1947.
Kurtz, Harold, *The Second Reich.* Macdonald, London, 1970.
Lange, Annemarie, *Berlin: Capital of the GDR.* Dresden, 1971.

Laqueur, Walter, *Weimar: A Cultural History 1918-33.* Weidenfeld & Nicolson, London, 1974.
Masur, Gerhard, *Imperial Berlin.* Routledge & Kegan Paul, London, 1974.
Nelson, Walter Henry, *The Berliners.* Longmans, London, 1969.
Schneider, Richard, *Das Neue Berlin-Buch.* Nicolai, Berlin, 1976.
Smith, Jean Edward, *The Defense of Berlin.* Johns Hopkins Press, Baltimore, 1963.
Sontheimer, Kurt, and Bleek, Wilhelm, *The Government and Politics of East Germany.* Hutchinson University Library, London, 1975.
Speer, Albert, *Inside the Third Reich.* Weidenfeld & Nicolson, London, 1970.
Terveen, Frederick, *Berlin in Photograpien des 19. Jahrhunderts.* Rembrandt, Berlin, 1968.

Acknowledgements and Picture Credits

The authors and editors wish to thank the following for their valuable assistance: H. L. Blackmore, H.M. Tower of London; Charles Dettmer, Thames Ditton, Surrey; Embassy of the German Democratic Republic, London; Manfred Füger, Senat für Wirtschaft, Berlin; Goethe Institute, London; Jim Hicks, London; Frau Rosa Jahn, Frankfurt-am-Main; Dr. Roland Klemig, Staatsbibliothek, Berlin; Norman Kolpas, London; Janet Langmaid, the Wiener Library, London; Marilyn Morfill Parker, London; Karin Pearce, London; Willa Petschek, London; Udo Polczynski, London; the Press and Information Office of Land Berlin, London; Hans Tasiemka, London; John Willett, London; Verkehrsamt, Berlin.

Sources for pictures in this book are shown below. Credits for the pictures from left to right are separated by commas; from top to bottom they are separated by dashes.

All photographs are by Leonard Freed from Magnum Photos except: Front end paper—Ludwig Windstosser. Page 6—Thomas Höpker. 10, 11—Map by Hunting Surveys Ltd., London, (Silhouettes by Anna Pugh). 14, 15—Frederic V. Grunfeld. 16—*Das grosse Zille-Album,* Büchergilde Gutenberg, Frankfurt-am-Main. Copyright: Fackelträger Verlag, Hannover. 17—Ludwig Windstosser. 19, 38—Frederic V. Grunfeld. 40, 41 —Ludwig Windstosser. 48, 49—Max Jacoby. 68, 69, 72—Frederic V. Grunfeld. 74 to 85—Landesbildstelle, Berlin, except 82 (inset)—Bildarchiv Preussischer Kulturbesitz, Staatsbibliothek, Berlin. 95—(left) Bildarchiv Preussischer Kulturbesitz, Staatsbibliothek, Berlin, (top)—Thomas Höpker. 100, 101—Ullstein, Berlin. 120—Bildarchiv Preussischer Kulturbesitz, Staatsbibliothek, Berlin. 121—Landesbildstelle, Berlin—Associated Press, London. 128, 129—Thomas Höpker. 133, 136 (top)—Frederic V. Grunfeld. 136 (bottom)— Thomas Höpker. 137—Frederic V. Grunfeld. 140, 141—Thomas Höpker. 152—Bildarchiv Preussischer Kulturbesitz, Staatsbibliothek, Berlin. 154, 155—Frederic V. Grunfeld. 157—montage of photographs from Bildarchiv Preussischer Kulturbesitz, Staatsbibliothek, Berlin. 160—Collection Gunn Brinson. 162, 163—Courtesy of Frau Martha Dix, and Galerie der Stadt, Stuttgart. Photo Liedtke & Michel, Stuttgart. 165—Ullstein, Berlin. 166—Ludwig Windstosser. 169—Collection Gunn Brinson. 178, 179—Stern Magazine. 185—Thomas Höpker. 190—Max Jacoby. 195, 196, 197 and last end paper—Thomas Höpker.

Index

Numerals in italics indicate a photograph or drawing of the subject mentioned.

Colour reproduction by Irwin Photography Ltd., at their Leeds PDI Scanner Studio.
Filmsetting by C. E. Dawkins (Typesetters) Ltd., London, SE1 1UN.
Printed and bound in Italy by Arnoldo Mondadori, Verona.